PREFACE

In this, my book, I have endeavored to give expression to the art of cookery as developed in recent years in keeping with the importance of the catering business, in particular the hotel business, which, in America, now leads the world.

I have been fortunate in studying under the great masters of the art in Europe and America; and since my graduation as Chef I have made several journeys of observation to New York, and to England, France and Switzerland to learn the new in cooking and catering.

I have named my book The Hotel St. Francis Cook Book in compliment to the house which has given me in so generous measure the opportunity to produce and reproduce, always with the object of reflecting a cuisine that is the best possible.

Victor Hirtzler.

JANUARY 1

BREAKFAST
  Sliced oranges
  Farina with cream

LUNCH
  Eggs Oriental
  Tripe and potatoes, family style

Calf's liver and bacon	Cold ham and tongue
Lyonnaise potatoes	Celery root, field and beet salad
Rolls	Port de Salut cheese
Coffee	Crackers
	Coffee

DINNER

Consommé d'Orleans
Boiled whitefish, Netherland sauce
Squab pot pie, à l'Anglaise
Lettuce and tomatoes, mayonnaise
Savarin Montmorency
Demi tasse

EggsOriental. Put on a plate one slice of tomato fried in butter, on top of the tomato place six slices of cucumber simmered in butter and well seasoned, on top of that one poached egg, and cover with sauce Hollandaise.

Tripeandpotatoes,familystyle. Slice the white ends of six leeks very fine, put in sauce pan with four ounces of butter and simmer for five minutes. Then add a scant spoonful of flour and simmer again. Then add one pound of tripe cut in pieces one inch square, one pint of bouillon, two raw potatoes sliced fine, some chopped parsley, salt and pepper, and one-half glass of white wine. Cover and cook for an hour, or until all is soft.

Boiledwhitefish,Netherlandstyle. Boil, and serve on napkin with small boiled potatoes, lemon and parsley. Serve melted butter separate.

Squabpotpie,àl'Anglaise. Roast the squabs and cut in two. Fry a thin slice of fillet of beef on both sides, over a quick fire, in melted butter. Put both in a pie dish with a chopped shallot that was merely heated with the fillet, six heads of canned or fresh mushrooms, one-half of a hard-boiled egg, a little chopped parsley, and some flour gravy made from the roasted squab juice, and well seasoned with a little Worcestershire sauce. Cover with pie dough and bake for twenty minutes. This is for an individual pie; make in the same proportions for a large pie.

Lemonwaterice.   One quart of water, one pound of sugar, and four lemons. Dissolve the sugar in the water, add the rinds of two lemons and the juice of four lemons. Strain and freeze.

Orangewaterice.   One quart of water, one pound of sugar, three oranges and one lemon. Melt the sugar in the water, add the juice of the oranges and the lemon, and one drop of coloring. Strain and freeze.

Strawberrywaterice.   One-half pound of sugar, one pint of water, one pint of strawberry pulp, the juice of one lemon, and coloring. Strain and freeze.

Raspberrywaterice.   Same directions as for strawberry water ice. Use raspberry pulp instead.

Cantaloupewaterice.   Add to one quart of cantaloupe pulp the juice of three lemons and a half pound of sugar. Pass through a fine sieve and freeze.

JANUARY2

BREAKFAST
  Grape nuts with cream
  Kippered herring
  Rolls
  Coffee

LUNCH
  Omelet with oysters
  Perch sauté, meunière
  Browned hashed potatoes
  Lobster salad with anchovies
  Floating island
  Napoleon cake
  Coffee

DINNER
  Little Neck clams
  Codfish chowder

        Planked shad and roe
        Artichokes au gratin
        Hearts of romaine, Roquefort dressing
        Peach Melba
        Caroline cakes
        Coffee

Omeletwithoysters. Parboil six oysters, add one spoonful of cream sauce and season well. Make the omelet, and before turning over on platter place the oysters in the center. Serve with light cream around the omelet.

Perchsauté,meunièr e. Season the fish well with salt and pepper, roll in flour, put in frying pan and cook with butter. When done, put fish on platter, and put a fresh piece of butter in pan, over fire, and allow to become hazelnut color. Pour the butter and the juice of a lemon over the fish, sprinkle with chopped parsley, and garnish with quartered lemons and parsley in branches.

Brownedhashedpotatoes. Hash three cold boiled potatoes. Melt three ounces of butter in a frying pan, add the potatoes, season with salt and pepper, and fry evenly. When nearly done form in the pan in the shape of a rolled omelet and fry again until well browned on the top. Turn over on platter in the same manner as an omelet, and sprinkle with chopped parsley.

Lobstersalad. Take the tails of two boiled lobsters, season with salt and pepper and a teaspoonful of vinegar, and let stand for a half hour, then add one cup of mayonnaise sauce. Put some sliced lettuce in the bottom of a salad bowl, the lobster salad on top, a few nice lettuce leaves around the sides, cover the salad again with mayonnaise, and decorate with hard-boiled eggs, beets and olives.

Lobstersaladwithanchovies. Same as above. Decorate with fillets of anchovies.

Floatingisland. Beat the whites of six eggs very stiff, add six ounces of powdered sugar and the inside of a vanilla bean. Mix well. Boil one quart of milk, one-quarter pound of sugar, and the remainder of the vanilla bean, in a wide vessel. Dip a tablespoon in hot water and form the beaten eggs, or meringue, into the shape and size of an egg, and drop into the boiling milk. Dip the spoon in hot water each time so the meringue will not stick. Take off the fire and let stand for a few minutes, turning the floating eggs several times. Then take out of the milk and dress on napkin to cool. Boil the milk again and bind with the yolks of two eggs, strain and cool. Put the sauce in a bowl, or deep dish, and float the "islands" on top. Serve very cold.

JANUARY 3

BREAKFAST
 Orange Juice
 Waffles and honey
 Chocolate and whipped cream

LUNCHEON
 Chicken salad, Victor
 Rolls
 Coffee

DINNER
 Potage Normande
 Fillet of turbot, Daumont
 Sirloin of beef, Clermont
 Endives salad
 Rolled oats pudding
 Coffee

Chicken salad, Victor. Cut the breast of a boiled soup hen or boiled chicken in half-inch squares, add one-half cup of string beans cut in pieces one inch long, a cup of boiled rice, one peeled tomato cut in small squares and one sliced truffle. Season with salt, fresh-ground black pepper, a little chives, chervil, parsley, one spoonful of tarragon vinegar and two spoonsful of best olive oil. Mix well and serve on lettuce leaves.

Potage Normande. Velouté with Julienne of carrots and turnips.

Fillet of turbot, Daumont. Put the fillet in a buttered pan, season with salt and pepper, and add one glass of white wine. Boil six fresh mushrooms in a little water and strain the juice over the fish, or use the juice of canned mushrooms. Cook the fish, remove to platter, and reduce the sauce to glace, then add one pint of sauce au vin blanc (white wine sauce), strain, and before pouring over the fish add two ounces of sweet butter and the juice of one lemon.

Sirloin of beef, Clermont. Roast sirloin of beef, sauce Madère, garnished with tomatoes stuffed with whole chestnuts, and Bermuda onions stuffed with cabbage.

Boiled chestnuts. Cut the chestnut shells with a sharp knife and put on pan in oven for ten minutes. Then peel, put in vessel with a small piece of celery, salt, and cover with water. Boil slowly so they will remain whole when done. Use for garnishing, stuffing, etc.

Tomatoes stuffed with chestnuts. Peel four nice fresh tomatoes, cut off the tops, scoop out the insides, and fill with boiled chestnuts. Put a small piece of butter on top, and put in oven for five minutes. Serve as a garnish, or as an entrée with Madeira sauce.

Boiled cabbage. Cut a head of cabbage in four, trim and wash well. Have a kettle with salt water boiling. Put the cabbage in the kettle and cook until nearly soft, then drain off nine-tenths of the water, add a small piece of ham, or ham bone, and simmer till soft. Remove the ham or bone and prepare the cabbage with cream, or any other style. For stuffing onions, cut the cabbage up, add a little butter, and season with salt and pepper.

Stuffed onions with cabbage. Peel four large Bermuda or Spanish onions. Boil them in salt water until nearly done, then remove from the fire and allow to cool. Take out the inside and fill with cabbage prepared as above. Put the stuffed onions on a buttered dish with a piece of butter on top, and bake in oven.

JANUARY 4

BREAKFAST
Hothouse raspberries with cream
Baked beans, Boston style
Brown bread
Coffee

LUNCHEON
Canapé of fresh caviar
Consommé Julienne
Boiled Salmon, sauce Princess
Corned beef hash with poached eggs
Escarole salad
French pastry   Coffee

DINNER
Lynn Haven oysters
Strained chicken okra, in cups
Cheese straws
Salted English walnuts
Fillet of sole, Gasser
Stuffed capon, St. Antoine
Asparagus Hollandaise
Gauffrette potatoes
Season salad   Coupe St. Jacques
Assorted cakes   Coffee

Consommé Julienne. The word "Julienne" is a common kitchen term, signifying cut in slender strips, or match shape. For consommé garnish cut "Julienne" style one carrot, one turnip, one leek, a small piece of celery, four leaves of cabbage, and one-half of an onion. Season with a spoonful of salt, and one-half teaspoonful of sugar. Mix well. Put in a well-buttered casserole, cover with buttered paper and the casserole cover, put in oven moderately hot, and allow to simmer slowly. Turn occasionally, using a fork to avoid breaking the vegetables. They should simmer without adding liquid, but should they be too dry, a half cup of consommé may be added. Cook until soft, and drain on a sieve so all the juice will run off. Combine with two quarts of consommé, and before serving add a few peas and some chervil.

Fillet of sole, Gasser. Put four fillets of sole in cold milk seasoned with salt and pepper, and leave for four hours. Then wrap around raw potatoes, cut like a cork, and about three inches long. Let one side extend over the potato, and fasten with a toothpick. Fry slowly in swimming lard until golden brown, then take out, remove the toothpick, push out the potato, and fill the center of the sole with a very thick filling composed of two-thirds Béarnaise sauce and one-third of reduced tomato sauce. Serve on napkin with fried parsley, and tomato sauce, separate.

Boiled salmon, sauce Princess. Boil the salmon, serve the sauce separate. Make the sauce as follows: One pint of Hollandaise sauce, one spoonful of meat extract, and twelve parboiled oysters, thoroughly mixed.

Stuffed capon, St. Antoine. Season the capon well, both inside and out, and put in ice box. Prepare a stuffing as follows: The bread crumbs made from a five-cent loaf of bread, twelve whole boiled chestnuts, three boiled fresh, or canned, apricots, six stewed prunes, three boiled, or canned, pears, and two peaches. Put in a bowl, add an egg and one gill of brandy, and mix well. Fill the capon, wrap a piece of fat pork around it, and put in roasting pan with a carrot, onion, bouquet garni, and three ounces of butter. Put in oven and roast slowly, basting continually until done. Remove the capon to a platter and take off the fat pork. Return the pan to fire and bring to a boil. When the fat is clear drain it off and add to the pan one-half cup of bouillon and one cup of brown gravy. Season, boil, strain and pour over the capon. Garnish with watercress.

JANUARY 5

BREAKFAST	LUNCHEON
Baked apples with	Shirred eggs, Mornay

cream
Fried hominy
Maple syrup
Coffee

Fried smelts, Tartar
Broiled spareribs and sauerkraut
Plain boiled potatoes
American cheese and crackers
Coffee

DINNER

Potage Marquis
Celery
Stuffed lobster
Boiled beef, sauce piquante
Maître d'hôtel potatoes
Brussels sprouts and chestnuts
Spinach, English style
Savarin Mirabelle
Coffee

Shirred eggs, Mornay. Put on a buttered shirred egg dish one spoonful of cream sauce, break two fresh eggs on top, season with salt and pepper, cover the eggs with sauce Mornay, sprinkle with grated cheese and bake in oven.

Potage Marquis. Cream of rice with breast of boiled chicken cut in small squares.

Stuffed lobster. Prepare the lobster as for croquettes. Clean the shells and fill with the prepared lobster. Sprinkle the top with cheese and bread crumbs mixed with a small piece of butter, and bake in oven. Serve on napkin with quartered lemon and parsley.

Maître d'hôtel potatoes. Peel and slice two boiled potatoes and put in pan. Season with salt and pepper, cover with thick cream, and boil for a few minutes. Then add two ounces of sweet butter and mix well, being careful not to break the potatoes. Just before serving add the juice of one-half lemon and some chopped parsley.

Boiled Brussels sprouts. Clean and wash the sprouts, boil in salt water till soft. Drain and cool. Be careful that the sprouts remain whole.

Brussels sprouts with chestnuts. Melt three ounces of butter in pan, add two cups of fresh-boiled sprouts, season with salt and pepper, and fry for a few minutes. Then add a cup of fresh-boiled chestnuts, mix well, and serve with a sprinkle of parsley on top.

Boiled spinach. Clean the spinach and wash in four or five waters, as it is difficult to remove the sand. It is sometimes necessary to wash as many as ten times to remove it all. Put a gallon of water and a handful of salt in a pot and bring to the boiling point. Add the spinach, and boil over a very hot fire, so it will remain green. It will require from five to ten minutes, depending upon the tenderness of the spinach. Drain off water and serve plain. Or, cool with cold water, press dry with the hand, and prepare as desired.

Spinach, English style. Add a small piece of butter to plain spinach.

JANUARY 6

BREAKFAST
　Sliced pineapple
　Waffles
　Honey in comb
　Rolls
　Coffee

LUNCHEON
　Croquettes Liviannienne
　Eggs Beaujolais
　Camembert cheese and crackers
　Coffee

DINNER
　Potage Victoria
　Bass, Provençale
　Stuffed lamb chops, Maréchal

Curried Lima beans
Château potatoes
Lettuce salad
Nectarine ice cream
Assorted cakes
Coffee

Croquettes Liviannienne. Mix four leaves of melted gelatine with one pint of mayonnaise and use to bind some crab meat. Cool and form in small croquettes, roll in chopped yolks of hard-boiled eggs mixed with chopped parsley.

Eggs Beaujolais. Poached eggs on toast covered with sauce Colbert.

Potage Victoria. Half velouté of chicken and half purée of tomatoes. Garnish with turnip cut in small squares, string beans cut in half-inch lengths, and a few peas.

Bass, Provençale. Split a bass, remove the bones and skin, put in buttered pan, season with salt and pepper, put some sliced tomatoes and a few small pieces of butter on top, and bake in oven. When done cover with white wine sauce with a few pieces of tomato in it.

Stuffed lamb chops, Maréchal. Broil the lamb chops on one side. Cover that side with force meat of veal quenelles decorated with chopped tongue and truffles, put in buttered pan, cover with buttered paper, and bake in oven for ten minutes. Serve with fresh mushroom sauce. (See veal force meat recipe Jan. 11.)

Macédoine water ice. Two pounds of sugar, three quarts of water, and six lemons. Dissolve the sugar in the water, add the rind of four lemons and the juice of six, strain and freeze. When frozen add one quart of assorted fruit, such as small seedless grapes, stoned cherries, and apricots, strawberries, and pineapple cut in small dices, or any other kind in season, or canned. Before adding the fruit to the water ice put it in a bowl with a little powdered sugar and kirschwasser, and leave for an hour. This will prevent the fruit from freezing too hard.

Normandie water ice. Two pounds of sugar, two quarts of water, and the juice of six lemons. Mix together, add one quart of crabapple pulp and one gill of cognac. Freeze.

Curried Lima beans. Put some boiled Lima beans in a sauce pan and cover with well seasoned curry sauce. Before serving add a small piece of fresh butter and some chopped parsley.

JANUARY 7

BREAKFAST
  Stewed rhubarb
  Boiled eggs
  Dry toast
  Coffee

LUNCHEON
  Consommé favorite
  Broiled shad roe, maître d'hôtel
  Mirabeau salad
  Lemon pie
  Coffee

DINNER
  Potage à l'Anglaise
  Fillet of flounder, Meissonier
  Chicken, Valencienne
  Jets de houblons
  Sybil potatoes
  Hearts of romaine
  Macédoine water ice
  Lady fingers
  Coffee

Consommé favorite. Garnish the consommé with asparagus tips cut in small pieces, and chicken dumplings stuffed with goose liver, the size of a large olive. Teaspoons may be used to form the dumplings.

Broiled shad roe, maître d'hôtel. Season the roe well with salt and pepper, roll in olive oil, and broil. Serve with maître d'hôtel sauce, and garnish with quartered lemon and parsley.

Mirabeau salad. Cut in one-inch squares one cucumber, two tomatoes, and one potato. Put in salad bowl separately, cover with vinaigrette sauce. Add one teaspoonful of French mustard in the vinaigrette. Lay anchovies over the top, and a green olive cut in strips, in the middle.

Potage à l'Anglaise. Put in vessel two pounds of lean mutton, and one pound of barley. Cover with water, season with salt, add a bouquet garni, and boil for two hours. Then remove the bouquet and the meat, strain through a fine sieve, add one pint of boiling thick cream, three ounces of sweet butter, and a little Cayenne pepper.

Fillet of flounder, Meissonier. Cook the fillets in white wine. Make a white wine sauce and add a Julienne of vegetables, and pour over the fish before serving.

Chicken, Valencienne. Salt and pepper a jointed chicken and sauté in pan with butter. Put on platter and serve with suprême with truffles and fresh mushrooms, cut in small squares, and quenelles (chicken dumplings), teaspoon size. Garnish with heart-shaped fried crusts of bread.

Coupe St. Jacques. Slice some fresh fruits, such as oranges, pineapple, pears and bananas, and add all fresh berries in season. Put in a bowl with one-quarter pound of sugar, and a small glass of kirschwasser and of maraschino. Let stand for about two hours. Then fill coupe glasses about half full with the fruit, and fill the remainder with two kinds of water ice, raspberry and lemon. Smooth the top with a knife, and decorate with some of the fruit used for filling.

BREAKFAST	LUNCHEON
Baked apples	Hors d'oeuvres variés
Scrambled eggs with parsley	Pilaff à la Turc
Rolls	Pont l'Évêque cheese
Coffee	Crackers
	Fruit
	Coffee

DINNER
Potage Quirinal
Fillet of sole, Normande
Squab en compote
Artichoke Hollandaise
Peach ice cream
Pound cake
Coffee

Risotto. In a vessel put one chopped onion, two ounces of butter, and the marrow of a beef bone chopped fine; and simmer until the onions are done. Then stir in one pound of rice, and put in oven for five minutes. Then add one and one-half pints of bouillon and a pinch of salt, cover, and place in oven for twenty minutes. Add a half cup of grated cheese before serving.

Pilaff à la Turc. Make a ring of risotto on a round platter, and in center put some well-seasoned chickens' livers, sauté au Madère.

Potage Quirinal. Make in the same manner as purée of game, but use pheasants only. Garnish with Julienne of breast of pheasants, truffles, and some dry sherry. Season with Cayenne pepper.

Fillet of sole, Normande. Cook the fillets "au vin blanc." Garnish individually with mussels, oysters, mushrooms, small Parisian potatoes, and very small fried fish. If small fish are not obtainable cut a fillet of sole in strips one-quarter-inch thick and two inches long, breaded and fry. Before serving place a slice of truffle on top of each piece of sole.

Peach ice cream. One pint of cream, one quart of milk, the yolks of eight eggs, one-half pound of sugar, one pint of peach pulp, and a few drops of peach kernel extract. Put the milk and one-half of the sugar on the fire to boil. Mix the other half of the sugar with the eggs, stir into the boiling milk, and cook until it becomes creamy, but do not let it come to the boiling point after adding the eggs. Remove from the fire, add the cream, pulp and extract, and freeze.

Banana ice cream. Same as the above, except substitute the pulp of six bananas and extract, in place of the peach pulp.

Pineapple ice cream. Add one pint of finely cut pineapple instead of the peach pulp.

Hazelnut ice cream. Roast one-half pound of hazelnuts, pound to a fine paste, mix with a little milk and two ounces of sugar. Use instead of the peach pulp.

Raspberry ice cream. Use one pint of raspberry pulp in place of the peach pulp.

JANUARY 9

BREAKFAST	LUNCHEON
Preserved figs with cream	Omelet with soft clams
Waffles	Ripe olives
Coffee	Broiled Spanish mackerel, fine herbs
	Hollandaise potatoes
	Cucumber salad
	German huckleberry pie

Coffee

DINNER

Bisque of California oysters

Salted pecans

Frogs' legs, Michels

Roast pheasant, bread sauce and bread crumbs

Compote of spiced peaches

Sweet potatoes, southern style

Asparagus, Polonaise

Banana ice cream

Lady fingers

Coffee

Omelet with soft clams. Take the bellies of six soft clams and put in pan, season with salt and pepper, add a small piece of butter, and heat through. Mix with two spoonsful of cream sauce. Make an omelet, and garnish with the clams in cream.

Broiled Spanish Mackerel, aux fines herbes. Season the mackerel with salt and pepper, roll in oil, and broil. Prepare a maître d'hôtel sauce with chopped chervil and chives, and pour over the fish. Garnish with quartered lemon and parsley in branches.

Cucumber salad. Slice some iced cucumbers and serve with French dressing. Or: Slice a cucumber and put in salad bowl, salt well and let stand for an hour, then squeeze the salt water out gently, and use dressing desired, as French dressing, Thousand Island dressing, etc. Or: Slice the cucumbers, cover with very thick cream, season with salt and paprika, and just before serving add the juice of one lemon.

Bisque of California oysters. Put one pint of California oysters, with their juice, in a pot and bring to the boiling point. Then skim, and add one pint of cream sauce, one-half pint of milk, a bouquet garni, and boil for ten minutes. Remove the bouquet garni, strain the broth through a fine sieve and return to the pot. Heat a pint of cream and strain into the soup, add three ounces of sweet butter, and season to taste.

Roastpheasant. Pheasant should be kept one week to season, before cooking. Clean, wrap in a slice of fresh lard, and roast in the same manner as chicken. Serve bread sauce and fried bread crumbs separate.

Breadsauce. Boil one cup of milk, add half of an onion, a little salt, one-third of a cup of fresh bread crumbs, and boil for five minutes. Remove the onion, add a piece of butter the size of a walnut, and season with Cayenne pepper.

Breadcrumbs. Put in frying pan three ounces of butter and three-quarters of a cup of fresh bread crumbs, and fry until brown. Then drain off the butter and serve the dry crumbs in a sauce boat.

JANUARY 10

BREAKFAST
- Oatmeal with cream
- Rolls
- Coffee

LUNCHEON
- Oysters Yaquino
- Cold assorted meats
- Potato salad
- Brie cheese and crackers
- Oolong tea

DINNER
- Potage Grande Mère
- Cold goosebreast with jelly
- Fillet of sole, royale
- Plain potted squab chicken
- Potatoes à la Reine
- Stuffed fresh mushrooms
- Hearts of romaine salad
- Pineapple ice cream

Assorted cakes

Coffee

Oysters Yaquino. Season one dozen oysters on the deep shell, with salt and paprika, put on each a piece of butter and some chopped chives. Place in oven, bake, and serve very hot.

Potage Grande Mère. Take equal parts of leeks, cabbage, onions and celery and cut in very small dices. Put in pot, cover with water, season with salt and pepper, and boil. When soft, add hot milk, and serve.

Fillet of sole, royale. Same as fillet of sole, Joinville.

Potted squab chicken. Prepare the chicken as for roasting. Season well, and put a small piece of fresh butter in each. Place in a sauté pan with butter and a piece of onion, brown well, basting from time to time. When almost done drain off the butter, add a cup of stock and a little brown gravy, and finish roasting. Strain the gravy over the chicken when serving. Serve in a casserole.

Potatoes à la Reine. Mix well, one cup of boiling water, one ounce of butter, and a half cup of flour; cool a little, and add the yolks of two eggs. Mix this dough with equal parts of fresh-boiled potatoes passed through a fine sieve, season with salt and a little grated nutmeg. Take up, with a spoon, in pieces the size of an egg, and drop one by one in warm swimming lard, heating gradually, so the potato will have time to swell (souffle), before becoming a golden brown color. When done, salt, and serve on napkin.

D'Uxelles. Put in flat sauce pan three ounces of butter, one chopped onion, and a slice of ham cut in small dices. Simmer for five minutes. Add the stems of fresh or canned mushrooms chopped very fine, and simmer again for five minutes; then add one-half glass of white wine and reduce. Then add one-half pint of brown gravy and boil for ten minutes. Finally stir in one-half cup of fresh bread crumbs, the yolks of two eggs, and season with salt and Cayenne pepper, and chopped parsley. D'Uxelles is used for garnishing in many ways.

Stuffed fresh mushrooms. Cut the stems from six fresh mushrooms, wash the heads well, season with salt and pepper, and fill with D'Uxelles. Place on a buttered dish, sprinkle with grated cheese, put a piece of butter on the top of each, and bake in a moderate oven.

JANUARY 11

BREAKFAST
  Grapefruit juice
  Pettijohns with cream
  Crescents
  Cocoa

LUNCHEON
  Pancake Molosol
  Scotch consommé
  Sweetbread patties with cream
  Meringue glacée with raspberries
  Coffee

DINNER
  Blue Points on shell
  Potage Bagration
  Celery. Ripe olives
  Paupiette of flounder, Bignon
  Roast ribs of beef
  Anna potatoes
  New peas
  Escarole salad
  Bavarois au chocolat
  Assorted cakes
  Coffee

Pancake Molosol. Spread some very thin French pancakes with fresh Russian caviar, roll up, and cut in diamond shapes. Serve on napkin, garnished with leaves of lettuce filled with chopped onions, quartered lemons, and parsley in branches. The pancakes must be fresh.

Scotch consommé. Boil a piece of mutton very slowly in consommé. When done strain the broth, add the mutton, cut in small dices, some brunoise, and some boiled barley.

Sweetbread patties with cream. Cut some parboiled sweetbreads in small dices and simmer a few minutes with a piece of butter. Add a little cream and cream sauce, season with salt and Cayenne pepper, boil for ten minutes. Have some hot patty shells, and fill.

Potage Bagration. Add to cream of chicken some boiled macaroni cut in pieces one-quarter inch in length.

Paupiette of flounder, Bignon. Stuff some fillets with fish force meat. Bread, and fry. Serve tomato sauce separate.

Fish forcemeat. Quarter pound trimmings of fish chopped fine, passed through sieve, and add one yolk of egg and a tablespoonful of cream. Salt and pepper.

Veal forcemeat. Quarter pound raw veal chopped fine, passed through sieve; add one raw yolk of egg, salt and pepper, and tablespoonful of cream.

Chicken forcemeat. Quarter pound raw chicken meat, chopped fine, and passed through sieve. Add one yolk of egg and a tablespoonful of cream. Salt and white pepper.

Anna potatoes. Peel some potatoes to a round shape, about the size of a dollar, and slice very thin, like Saratoga chips. Season with salt and pepper. Melt some butter in a round mould or hot frying pan, and lay the potatoes around the bottom; add layer upon layer until they are about two inches in height. Put some melted butter over them, and bake in a moderate oven for about a half hour. Drain off the butter and turn out upon a napkin on a platter.

Meringue glacée, with raspberries. Fill meringue shells with raspberry ice cream and garnish with fresh raspberries.

JANUARY 12

BREAKFAST
　Stewed prunes
　Boiled eggs
　Dry toast
　Coffee

LUNCHEON
　Eggs Mirabeau
　Hasenpfeffer (hare stew)
　Noodles
　Coffee éclairs
　Rolls
　Tea

DINNER
　Consommé d'Artagnan
　Pickles
　New England boiled dinner
　Apple pie
　Coffee

EggsMirabeau. Place some stuffed eggs in a buttered shirred egg dish, cover with cream sauce, and bake in oven.

Hasenpfeffer(har estew). Cut up a hare in three-inch pieces. Save the blood and liver in separate dish. Put the cut up meat in an earthen pot and cover with one-half claret, or white wine, and one-half water. Add one sliced carrot, one sliced onion, a bouquet garni with plenty of thyme in it, salt, and a spoonful of whole black peppers. Let stand for forty-eight hours, then drain, strain the juice, and put the meat on a platter. Put in a pan on the stove one-half pound of butter; when hot add two heaping spoonsful of flour, and allow to become nice and yellow, stirring all the while to prevent its burning. Then add the pieces of hare and simmer for a few minutes; then add the juice and a glass of water or bouillon, bring to the boiling point, cover and let simmer slowly. Parboil and fry in butter one dozen small onions; also cut up one-half pound of salt pork in half-inch squares, and parboil and fry them. When stew is about three-quarters cooked, add the onions, pork, and a can of French mushrooms, and cook until done. Now chop the liver fine, mix with the blood, and stir into the stew just before removing from the fire. Do not let it boil after adding the liver. Season to taste, and serve with a sprinkle of chopped parsley.

Consommé d'Artagnan. In the bottom of a buttered pan place one sliced carrot, one onion, a stalk of celery, a piece of raw ham, a sprig of thyme, one bay leaf, and some pepper berries. On top place three calf's feet, and simmer for a few minutes. Then add one-half glass of white wine and one-half glass of sherry, and three quarts of bouillon or stock. Clarify with the whites of six eggs, bringing to a boil slowly. Cook until the feet are soft. Strain the broth through cheese cloth, cut the calf's feet in small pieces and add to the consommé.

New England boiled dinner. Put a shoulder of salt pork in a pot, cover with water, bring to a boil, and then allow to become cool. Then put the pork in a pot with five pounds of brisket of beef, cover with water, add a little salt, a bouquet garni, three whole turnips, three beets, three carrots and a small head of cabbage. Cook until the vegetables are soft, then remove, and continue cooking the meat until well done. Place the meat on a platter, slice, and place the vegetables around the meat; add some plain boiled potatoes, pour a little of the broth over all, and serve hot.

JANUARY 13

BREAKFAST
- Stewed rhubarb
- Broiled finnan haddie
- Baked potatoes
- Rolls
- Coffee

LUNCHEON
- Oyster stew
- Eggs Gambetta
- Mutton chops
- French fried potatoes
- String beans
- Camembert cheese and crackers
- Coffee

DINNER
 Potage Venitienne
 Aiguillettes of bass, à la Russe
 Beef steak, Provençale
 Georgette potatoes
 Lettuce and tomato salad
 Fancy ice cream
 Assorted cakes
 Coffee

Oyster stew . Put in a pot six oysters with their own juice, bring to the boiling point, and skim. Then add one cup of boiling milk, one ounce of sweet butter, and salt. Serve crackers separate.

Eggs Gambetta. Dip four cold poached eggs in some beaten eggs, then in bread crumbs, and fry in swimming fat. Place on toast, garnish with boiled calf's brains and sliced truffles, and serve with Madeira sauce.

Potage V enitienne. Beat two spoonfuls of farina, two whole eggs and a half cup of milk together, stir into one quart of boiling consommé, and cook for twelve minutes.

Aiguillettes of bass, à la Russe. Remove the skin from the fillets of bass, and cut in slices (aiguillettes) about one and one-half inches wide and five inches long. Place in a buttered pan, season with salt and pepper, place on each piece three or four round slices of cooked carrots, add half a glass of white wine, cover with buttered paper, and cook slowly. Add some finely cut chervil to some white wine sauce, and pour over the fish.

Beefsteak, Pr ovençale. Cook a small sirloin steak sauté in butter, and season well. Cover one-half of the steak with Béarnaise sauce, and the other half with Béarnaise sauce mixed with a little puree of tomatoes. On top of each half place a round potato croquette the size of a walnut, and some Julienne potatoes around the steak.

Béarnaise sauce. Put in a sauce pan six very finely-chopped shallots, a spoonful of crushed white peppers, and a glass of tarragon vinegar, and reduce until nearly dry. Then put the pan in another vessel containing hot water, add the yolks of five eggs and stir in well. Then add one pound of sweet butter cut in small pieces. Stir the butter in piece by piece, and as it melts the sauce will become thick, like mayonnaise. Be careful that the sauce does not become too hot. Salt, strain through cheese cloth, add one teaspoonful of melted meat extract, some chopped fresh tarragon, and a little Cayenne pepper.

Béarnaisetomatée. One cup of thick puree of tomatoes mixed with two cups of Béarnaise sauce.

Choronsauce. Same as Béarnaise tomatée.

JANUARY 14

BREAKFAST
  Grapefruit juice
  Grape-nuts with cream
  Rolls
  Coffee

LUNCHEON
  Barquette à l'aurore.
  Salmon steak with anchovies
  Baked potatoes
  Cheese cake
  Coffee

DINNER
  Consommé crème de volaille
  Salted English walnuts
  Frogs' legs, sauté à sec
  Lamb chops, sauce Soubise
  Stewed tomatoes
  Brussels sprouts
  Hearts of romaine
  Meringue Chantilly
  Coffee

Barquette à l'aurore. Small tartelettes filled with Italian salad and covered with pink mayonnaise sauce.

Italian salad. Use equal parts of carrots, turnips, string beans, and roast beef cut in small squares, and of boiled peas. Season with salt, pepper, tarragon vinegar and olive oil, and garnish with beets and flageolet beans.

Pink mayonnaise. Add to two cups of mayonnaise, one-half cup of cold purée of tomatoes.

Consommé crème de volaille. Put some very light chicken force meat (quenelle) in small round buttered timbale moulds, and cook in bain-marie (double boiler). When done, slice thin and serve in hot consommé. (See chicken force meat recipe Jan. 11.)

Cheesecake. One and one-half pounds of cottage cheese, one-half pound of sugar, one-half pound of butter, the yolks of five eggs, one-half pint of milk, the whites of three eggs well beaten, and some vanilla extract. Mix the butter with the sugar, then the cheese, and the yolks of the eggs, one by one. Then add the milk, flour, and vanilla, and finally the beaten whites of eggs should be stirred in very slowly. Pour on pie dish or pan lined with a thin tartelette dough, and bake in a moderate oven.

Sauce Soubise. Parboil six sliced onions, and then pour off the water. Put in vessel with cold water and salt, and boil till done. Drain off the water, pass the onions through a fine sieve, add one pint of cream sauce, mix well, and season with salt and Cayenne pepper.

Soubise (for stuffing crabs, etc.). Slice a dozen onions, put in vessel with cold water and salt, bring to the boiling point, and allow to cool. Then put the onions in a well buttered casserole, add a half-pound of parboiled rice, a little salt, and two ounces of butter. Cover with a buttered paper and the casserole cover, put in oven and cook until soft. Then strain through a fine sieve; put in a vessel and add two spoonsful of thick cream sauce, heat well, and bind with the yolks of four eggs, season with salt and Cayenne pepper, and allow to cool. When cold mix with a spoon, and use as needed.

JANUARY 15

BREAKFAST
Broiled Yarmouth bloaters
Lyonnaise potatoes
Corn muffins
Coffee

LUNCHEON
Grapefruit with cherries
Scrambled eggs, Turbico
Curried lamb with rice
Chocolate éclairs
Coffee

DINNER
Blue Point oysters
Potage Marie Louise
Salted hazelnuts
Fillet of sole, Castelanne
Squab en compote
Spinach
Endive salad, French dressing
Coupe St. Jacques
Assorted cakes
Coffee

Scrambled eggs, Turbico. Mix with six scrambled eggs one-half cup of Créole sauce.

Curried lamb with rice. Cut three pounds of shoulder and breast of lean lamb in pieces two and one-half inches square. Parboil and put on fire in cold water with one carrot, one onion, a bouquet garni, and salt. Boil until the lamb is done; remove the vegetables, and strain the broth. Put in another vessel three ounces of butter, melt, add two spoonsful of curry powder and two of flour, heat, then add a sliced apple and banana fried in butter, and one-half cup of chutney sauce. Boil for twenty minutes. Strain over the lamb, and serve with boiled rice.

Potage Marie Louise. Mix one quart of purée of white beans with one pint of thick consommé tapioca.

Fillet of sole, Castelanne.   Put six fillets in a buttered pan, season with salt and pepper, add one-half glass of white wine, cover, and bake in oven for ten minutes. Make on a round platter a border of boiled rice. Place the fillets in the center. Strain the fish broth, mix with Créole sauce, and pour over the fish, completely covering same.

Squab en compote.   Prepare four squab as for roasting, except the stuffing. Season well, and put in earthen pot with an onion, carrot, and two ounces of butter. Put in oven and roast well, basting continually so they will retain their juice. To a brown gravy, or sauce Madère, add the following: Eight small onions boiled and fried, eight heads of fresh mushrooms sautéed in butter, eight small boiled French carrots, and two small pickles cut in two. Serve with the squabs.

JANUARY 16

BREAKFAST
- Oatmeal with cream
- Boiled eggs
- Dry toast
- Chocolate

LUNCHEON
- Clam broth in cups
- Broiled striped bass
- Vogeleier omelet
- Field salad
- Tartelette au Bar le Duc
- Coffee

DINNER
- Consommé, de la mariée
- Boiled codfish, oyster sauce
- Roast ribs of beef
- Lima beans
- Potato croquettes
- Escarole and chicory salad

Savarin Montmorency

Coffee

Vogeleieromelet. Cut a roll in very thin slices, put in omelet pan with two ounces of butter, and fry until crisp. Add eight beaten eggs, with salt, pepper, and plenty of chives, and make into an omelet.

TarteletteauBarleDuc. Line the moulds with tartelette dough, fill with raw white beans, and bake. When the dough is done remove the beans, and fill the tartelettes with imported Bar le Duc jelly. Decorate with whipped cream.

Consommédelamariée. Boil one quart of consommé. Put the yolks of four eggs in a soup tureen and stir well, adding the consommé slowly. Season with a little Cayenne pepper.

Oystersauce. Parboil a dozen oysters in their own juice for two minutes. Then strain the broth through a napkin into one pint of cream or Allemande sauce, add the oysters, and season.

Limabeans. Boil the beans in salt water until soft, drain off, add sweet butter and a little pepper, and simmer for a few minutes. Serve with a sprinkle of chopped parsley.

Peasincr eam. Boil the peas in salt water until nearly done. Drain off the water and add just enough thick cream to wet them, and simmer for five minutes. Then add a cup of cream sauce and cook until the peas are very soft. Add a little salt and a pinch of sugar.

Coupeoriental. Slice some fresh fruit, such as oranges, pineapple, bananas, etc., add all kinds of berries in season, and put in a bowl with some sugar and a small glass of kirsch or maraschino. Allow to macerate for a couple of hours. Then fill coupe glasses half way to the top with the fruit, and fill the remainder with vanilla ice cream. Place a strawberry or cherry on top. Cook about one-quarter of a pound of sugar so that it will crack when cold. It will require about 310 degrees. Dip a tablespoon into it and shake it over a stick, to form filé sugar (commonly called spun sugar). Cut this sugar in pieces and form in the shape of a ball, and put on top of the cup before serving.

JANUARY 17

BREAKFAST
  Baked apples with cream
  Poached eggs on toast
  Puff paste crescents
  English breakfast tea

LUNCHEON
  Pain mane
  Cold roast beef
  Fresh vegetable salad
  Roquefort cheese and crackers
  Coffee

DINNER
  Potage Andalouse
  Ripe olives
  Fillet of Spanish mackerel, Montebello
  Olivette potatoes
  Leg of lamb, au jus
  Mixed string beans
  Tomato salad
  Vanilla custard pie
  Coffee

Pain mane. Small dinner rolls, split, toasted, and filled with a purée of sweet-and-sour bananas, and garnished with pimentos.

Fresh vegetable salad. For this salad use any kind of fresh vegetables in season, such as string beans, Lima beans, carrots, cauliflower, asparagus, Brussels sprouts, tomatoes, peas, boiled celery, boiled celery roots, spring turnips, Jerusalem artichokes, fresh buttons of artichokes, etc. Place them in separate bouquets in a salad bowl, and use French dressing, or any other dressing desired.

Potage Andalouse. To velouté of beef add some cooked tapioca.

Fillet of Spanish mackerel, Montebello. Put the fillets in a buttered dish, season with salt and a little Cayenne pepper, cover with buttered paper, and bake in oven. Dress on a platter, and cover with sauce Béarnaise tomatée.

Olivette potatoes. Cut potatoes with a Parisian potato spoon to the shape of an olive. Put in a vessel with cold water, bring to the boiling point, and drain. Melt some butter in a sauté pan, add the potatoes, and bake in oven until a nice golden brown. Drain off the butter, and season with salt.

Sweet potatoes, rissolées. Boil some small sweet potatoes. When done peel and put in a pan with butter, and roast until brown. Season with salt.

JANUARY 18

BREAKFAST
Baked beans, Boston style
Brown bread
Omelet with jelly
Coffee

LUNCHEON
Hors d'oeuvres variés
Consommé Impératrice
Beef steak, Foch
Gendarme potatoes
Lettuce salad
Meringue glacée au chocolat
Coffee

DINNER
Oysters on half shell
Crème Maintenon
Queen olives
Fillet of sole, Lord Curzon
Stuffed goose, with chestnuts
Apple sauce
Sweet potatoes, rissolées
Peas in cream
Cold asparagus, mustard sauce
Coupe Oriental
Assorted cakes
Coffee

Consommé Impératrice. Consommé garnished with small lobster dumplings and asparagus tips in equal parts, and a sprinkle of chopped chervil.

Beef steak, Foch. Use sirloin, tenderloin, or rump steak. Season well, and sauté in butter. Place on a platter and put a thick piece of parboiled beef marrow, with one fried egg, on top. Serve with the pan gravy.

Meringue glacée au chocolat. Fill two meringue shells with chocolate ice cream, place together, and decorate with whipped cream.

Crème Maintenon (soup). Three parts crème à la Reine soup, and one part thick consommé Brunoise.

Fillet of sole, Lord Curzon. Put six fillets in a buttered pan, season with salt and a teaspoonful of curry powder, add one-half glass of white wine, cover with buttered paper, and bake in oven. When done put the fish on a platter, strain the broth into a pint of white wine sauce, add one chopped shallot, one tomato cut in squares, one red pepper, and two fresh mushrooms cut in squares and simmered in butter. Mix, season well, and pour over the fish.

Stuffed goose with chestnuts. Clean a goose, and keep the liver and gizzard. Fill with a chestnut stuffing, put in a roasting pan, salt, add a spoonful of water and place in the oven. The water will soon evaporate and the fat begin to melt. Baste well until the goose is done. Then remove the goose to a platter; save the grease for other purposes; and add to the pan one-half glass of bouillon or stock, and one spoonful of meat extract. Boil for five minutes. Serve the gravy separately. Also serve giblet sauce and apple sauce separately. The goose should be served very hot.

JANUARY 19

BREAKFAST
  Hothouse raspberries in cream
  Scrambled eggs with

LUNCHEON
  Consommé in cups
  Ripe California olives

bacon

Dry toast

Coffee

Broiled fillet of sole, maître d'hôtel

Cucumber salad

Deviled turkeys' legs, with chow chow

Mashed potatoes au gratin

Brie cheese and crackers

Coffee

DINNER

Potage gentilhomme

Fish dumplings, cream sauce

Small tenderloin steak, Florentine

Romaine salad, Roquefort dressing

English breakfast tea ice cream

Assorted cakes

Coffee

Deviled turkey's legs, with chow chow. Use the legs from a boiled or roasted turkey. Season with salt and pepper, spread some French mustard all over the surface, roll in bread crumbs, and broil; or fry in pan with a piece of butter. When nice and brown dish up on platter, and garnish with large leaves of lettuce filled with chow chow.

Mashed potatoes au gratin. Put some mashed potatoes in a buttered shirred egg dish or pie plate. Sprinkle with grated Parmesan or Swiss cheese, put small bits of butter on top, and bake until brown.

Potage gentilhomme. Potato soup with Julienne of carrots.

Julienne. Julienne is the term used in cooking for vegetables, or any kind of meat, etc., cut in long strips, like matches. Vegetable Julienne should be prepared and cooked as follows: Cut the vegetables in strips, add salt and a very little sugar, put in a well-buttered casserole, cover with buttered paper and the casserole cover. Put in oven and smother until soft. Turn gently once or twice, with a fork, so as not to break the vegetables.

Small tenderloin steak, Florentine. Broiled tenderloin steak, with sauce Madere, or brown sauce. Garnish with risotto, and just before serving garnish the risotto with truffles, ham and tongue cut in small squares.

Roquefort dressing, for salads. For four persons take four ounces of Roquefort cheese, put in salad bowl and mash well with a fork. Add one-half teaspoonful of salt, two pinches of ground black pepper, two tablespoonsful of vinegar, and three tablespoonsful of olive oil. Mix well and pour over the salad. If desired, one teaspoonful of Worcestershire sauce and a pinch of paprika may be added.

English breakfast tea ice cream. Prepare in the same manner as vanilla ice cream. Before freezing add some strong tea made of one ounce of English breakfast tea and one cup of boiling water.

JANUARY 20

BREAKFAST
　Stewed rhubarb
　Boiled eggs
　Buttered toast
　Coffee

LUNCHEON
　Eggs Oudinot
　Fricassee of veal, with noodles
　Chocolate profiteroles
　Coffee

DINNER
　Potage McDonald
　Lyon sausage
　Fried chicken, Maryland
　Cheese cake
　Coffee

Eggs Oudinot. Put some stuffed eggs in a shirred egg dish, cover with cream sauce, sprinkle with the chopped yolks of hard-boiled eggs, put a small piece of butter on the top of each, and bake in oven until brown.

Fricassee of veal. Cut five pounds of shoulder and breast of veal in pieces two and one-half inches square, put on fire in cold water, bring to the boiling point, and then cool. Put back in vessel, cover with water, add one carrot, one onion, a bouquet garni, a little salt, and boil until soft. Remove the vegetables and bouquet, and use the broth to make the fricassee sauce. Put in casserole on stove, six ounces of butter, when hot add three-quarters cup of flour, heat through, then add three pints of the veal broth, stir well and boil for ten minutes, then bind with the yolks of three eggs and a cup of cream. Season and strain the sauce over the pieces of veal. Allow to stand five minutes before serving. Noodles, spaghetti, or other paste, should be served, either separate or on the side of plate with the stew.

Noodle dough. Mix one pound of flour with five whole eggs, with a very little or no salt, and a pony of kirschwasser, if desired. Mix well, roll out very thin, and then let the dough become nearly dry. Then cut in strips. Have a vessel on the fire, with about a gallon and a half of boiling water. Add the noodles, and boil for seven minutes over a quick fire, so they will not stick together. Drain off the water and pour two ounces of hot melted butter over the noodles. A little grated nutmeg may be added, if desired. Noodles, like macaroni, may be prepared in many ways.

Chocolate profiteroles. Make some small cream puffs and fill with whipped cream. Place on a deep dish and cover with a sauce made of one pint of water, one-half pound of sugar, and three ounces of cocoa. Boil the water with the sugar, then add the cocoa and stir well. Boil for five minutes.

Potage McDonald. Boil one calf's brains in chicken broth. Make one quart of cream of barley soup, and strain both together through a fine sieve. Put in vessel and add one ounce of sweet butter, and, when melted, serve. Do not let the soup boil after the two have been joined.

Fried chicken, Maryland. Cut up a spring chicken, put in flour, then in eggs, and then in bread crumbs. Season with salt and pepper. Melt three ounces of butter in a frying pan, and when hot add the breaded chicken and fry until golden brown, but be careful not to burn it. It will require about twelve minutes for a young chicken. When done, put on platter with cream sauce over the bottom, and garnish with four corn fritters, four small potato croquettes the size of an ordinary cork, and four strips of fried bacon on top.

JANUARY 21

BREAKFAST
  Preserved figs
  Oatmeal with cream
  Rolls
  Cocoa

LUNCHEON
  Eggs Mery
  Roast fresh leg of pork, au jus
  Apple sauce
  Spinach
  Swiss cheese
  Crackers
  Coffee

DINNER
  Petite marmite
  Radishes
  Boiled beef, horseradish sauce
  Boiled potatoes
  Pickled beets
  Apple Charlotte
  Coffee

Eggs Mery. Scramble eight eggs, well seasoned. Just before they are done add one sliced truffle and two sliced pimentos. Serve in croustades.

Roast leg of fresh pork. Put on bottom of roasting pan one sliced carrot, one onion, three bay leaves, six cloves, one spoonful of pepper berries, and a piece of celery. Season the leg of pork with salt and pepper, and a little sage, if desired. Put on top of the vegetables, and place in oven to roast. Baste well. When done take out the pork, remove the fat in the pan, and add to the gravy a cup of stock or bouillon, and one tablespoonful of meat extract. Boil, strain, and season to taste.

Apple Charlotte. Chop six peeled apples and fry in butter with one-quarter pound of sugar, and one-half teaspoonful of ground cinnamon. Line a charlotte mould with slices of white bread cut as thin as possible, and buttered with fresh butter. Fill the mould with the fried apple and bake in oven for twenty-five minutes. Serve with brandy sauce.

JANUARY 22

BREAKFAST
  Stewed prunes
  Pettijohns with cream
  Rolls
  Coffee

LUNCHEON
  Canapé of fresh caviar
  Scrambled eggs with morilles
  Planked sirloin steak
  Romaine salad
  Camembert cheese
  Crackers
  Coffee

DINNER
  Consommé Bretonne
  Lyon sausage
  Lobster Thermidor
  Noisettes of lamb, Cendrillon
  Peas au beurre
  Celery mayonnaise
  Apple water ice
  Cakes
  Coffee

Scrambled eggs with morilles. Morilles are a species of mushroom rarely found in the United States. They come principally from Europe in cans, or dried. When fresh ones are used, sauté in butter and mix with the scrambled eggs. When in can, drain off the water, put in sauce pan with a piece of butter, season with salt and pepper, simmer for ten minutes, and add to the eggs. When dried, soak them in cold water over night, wash, and then proceed in the same manner as with the canned ones.

Planked sirloin steak. Broil the steak in the usual manner. When nearly done put on a meat plank, put four slices of broiled tomatoes on top, place four strips of broiled bacon across the tomatoes, and roast in oven for five minutes. Cover with maître d'hôtel sauce, and garnish with Parisian potatoes, parsley in branches, and quartered lemon.

Consommé Bretonne. Make a Julienne of equal parts of celery, onions and leeks, and serve in consommé.

Lobster Thermidor. Cut a live lobster in two lengthwise, sprinkle with olive oil, season with salt and pepper, and put in oven and bake. When done remove the meat from the shell and cut in small squares. Then make a sauce as follows: Chop two shallots, a little parsley and tarragon, add one spoonful of meat extract, or some good meat gravy, and reduce by boiling until nearly dry. Then add one spoonful of dry mustard, one cup of cream sauce, and two ounces of fresh butter. Put some of the sauce in the bottom of the shells, put the lobster in the sauce, and pour the remainder over the top. Sprinkle with grated cheese, and bake in oven until brown.

JANUARY 23

BREAKFAST
   Poached eggs on toast
   Broiled ham

LUNCHEON
   Mariniert herring
   Potato salad

Rolls　　　　　　　　　　　　　Lemon pie
Ceylon tea　　　　　　　　　　 Coffee

DINNER

California oyster cocktails
Bisque of crabs
Ripe olives
Frogs' legs, marinière
Roast chicken, au jus
Watercress salad
Asparagus Hollandaise
Peach Melba
Carolines (cakes)
Coffee

Bisque of crabs. Take two large raw Pacific crabs and put in vessel with cold water, season with salt and a bouquet garni, and boil for one-half hour. Then crack the shells and remove the meat. Use the meat for salad, an entrée dish, or to garnish the soup. Put the shell in a mortar and smash fine. In a vessel put one-quarter pound of butter and the broken shell, and simmer. Then add one pint of the water used to boil the crab, and one pint of milk, and boil for ten minutes. Then add one quart of cream sauce, boil again, and strain through a fine sieve. Put back in pot, add one pint of boiling thick cream, salt and Cayenne pepper, and just before serving add three ounces of sweet butter and one cup of crab meat cut in small pieces.

Cocktail sauce, for oysters (1) One cup of tomato ketchup, one pinch of salt, a little Cayenne pepper, paprika, and celery salt, one teaspoonful of Worcestershire sauce, and one tablespoonful of tarragon vinegar.

(2) One cup of tomato ketchup, one-half teaspoonful of paprika, one spoonful of grated horseradish sauce, salt, one spoonful of Worcestershire sauce, and the juice of one lemon.

Oyster cocktail. Use California oysters, Toke Points, Blue Points, Lynnhavens, Seapuits, or any other kind. Put in an oyster cocktail glass and mix with plenty of cocktail sauce. Set the glass in ice, and serve with lemons cut in half.

Frogs' legs, marinière. Cut the hind legs of two dozen small frogs in two. Put in sauté pan with three ounces of butter, season with salt and pepper, and simmer for five minutes. Then add six chopped shallots and simmer for three minutes. Then one-half glass of white wine and boil until nearly dry. Then add one pint of Allemande sauce, fricassee sauce, or sauce au vin blanc, and boil for five minutes. Serve with a sprinkle of chopped chives and parsley over the top.

JANUARY 24

BREAKFAST
  Preserved strawberries
  Finnan haddie in cream
  Baked potatoes
  Corn muffins
  Coffee

LUNCHEON
  Eggs Chipolata
  Tripe à la mode de Caën
  Chocolate éclairs
  Coffee

DINNER
  Consommé parfait
  Pimentos à l'huile
  Sand dabs, meunière
  Leg of lamb, Boulangère
  Chiffonade salad
  Rolled oats pudding
  Coffee

Eggs Chipolata. Make some shirred eggs and garnish with sauce Madère, to which has been added two small roasted onions, two heads of mushrooms, two small French carrots, three boiled chestnuts, and two very small fried sausages.

Consommé parfait. To one pint of lukewarm consommé tapioca add four raw beaten eggs, put in buttered mould, set in pan in boiling water, and put in moderate oven for ten minutes. Allow to cool, cut in slices, and serve in consommé.

Pimentos à l'huile. This is a plain hors d'oeuvres. Take a can of pimentos, drain off the juice, cut the pepper in four; place on a platter, season with salt and pepper, add one part vinegar and two parts olive oil, and sprinkle with chopped parsley.

Leg of lamb, Boulangère. Season a leg of lamb with salt and pepper, and rub with garlic and butter. Put in roasting pan with a cup of water and a bouquet garni. Slice two large onions very fine, also six raw potatoes the size of a silver dollar, mix, season with salt and pepper, and place around the leg of lamb. Put small pieces of butter on top, put in oven, and baste the meat only. It will require about one and one-quarter hours to cook. Do not disturb the potatoes while cooking. When done remove the bouquet garni, and serve the meat and potatoes very hot, with chopped parsley on top.

Rolled oats pudding. Boil one pint of milk with half of a split vanilla bean; add two ounces of rolled oats and two ounces of sugar, and cook for about ten minutes. Remove from the fire. Separate the yolks and whites of four eggs, add the yolks to the rolled oats and mix well. Beat the whites very hard with a whip, and add to the batter lightly. Put in buttered pudding mould and bake in bain-marie (hot water bath) for about thirty minutes. Take out of mould and serve with vanilla cream sauce.

Vanilla cream sauce. Boil one pint of milk with one-quarter of a split vanilla bean. Mix one-quarter of a pound of sugar with two eggs and one spoonful of sifted flour. Pour the boiling milk over this mixture, and put back on the fire, stir well, and allow to become thick. Then add one cup of cream, strain and serve.

Cream sauce (sweet—quick). One pint of cream, two ounces of sugar, and some flavoring. Mix well, and serve hot or cold.

JANUARY 25

BREAKFAST
 Oatmeal with cream
 Boiled eggs
 Dry toast
 Coffee

LUNCHEON
 Hors d'oeuvres variés
 Clam broth in cups
 Cheese straws
 Broiled lamb chops
 French fried potatoes
 Cold artichokes, mustard sauce
 Apple pie
 Coffee

DINNER
 Chicken okra
 Queen olives
 Fillet of sole, Rose Caron
 Vol au vent, Toulouse
 Roast saddle of venison
 Purée of chestnuts
 Peas au cerfeuil
 Sweet potatoes, Southern style
 Lettuce salad
 Omelette soufflé à la vanille
 Coffee

Fillet of sole, Rose Caron. Skin the four fillets of one large sole and place on a buttered pan. Put on top of each, three slices of cooked lobster, season with salt and paprika, add one-half glass of white wine, cover with buttered paper, put in oven and cook for twelve minutes. Remove the fillets to a platter, taking care that the lobster does not fall off. To the gravy in the pan add one pint of white wine sauce and boil for ten minutes, then add two tablespoonsful of écrevisse butter, and strain the sauce over the fish. Heat in sherry wine sixteen slices of truffles, and put four on top of each fillet, after the sauce has been added. Garnish with fleurons.

Sweet potatoes, Southern style. Peel and slice some boiled sweet potatoes and put in buttered shirred egg dishes, or pie plates. Add a little salt, molasses and maple syrup, sprinkle with powdered sugar, put some small bits of butter on top, and bake in oven until brown.

Vol au vent, or patty shells. Take some puff paste, with six turns, and roll out to about one-quarter inch in thickness. With a round pastry cutter about three inches in diameter, cut the paste. Then moisten with egg, and with the tip of a small knife trace a ring on each patty about one-half inch from the edge. Bake in a hot oven for about twenty minutes. Take out of the oven and with the knife point lift off the center cover within the traced circle, and empty of the uncooked paste inside.

Garniture Toulouse. Cut the garnishing to agree with the size of the patty. For the size described above cut in pieces about one-half inch square. For larger patties cut from an inch to an inch and a half square. Use the boiled breast of chicken, sweetbreads boiled in chicken broth, and French mushrooms in equal parts, one-half of a sliced truffle to each person, three chicken dumplings, teaspoon size cut in two, rooster kidneys and rooster combs. Mix well, and stew in a sauce Allemande made of chicken broth and well seasoned. Fill the hot patty shells and serve on platter, garnished with parsley in branches.

JANUARY 26

BREAKFAST
  Waffles
  Honey in comb
  Coffee

LUNCHEON
  Grapefruit with sherry
  Mixed grill
  Cup custard
  Lady fingers
  Coffee

DINNER

        Purée Crécy
        Radishes
        Bouillabaisse Marseillaise
        Roast leg of mutton, currant jelly
        String beans
        Hashed in cream potatoes
        Escarole salad
        Napoleon cake
        Coffee

Mixed grill. Broil one lamb chop, one breakfast sausage, one slice of tomato, one whole fresh mushroom head, and one whole lamb kidney. Put all on a plate, cover with maître d'hôtel sauce, and serve hot. Garnish with watercress.

Cup custard. Mix four eggs, one-quarter pound of sugar, one pint of milk, and flavor with vanilla. Strain, pour into cups, and bake in bain-marie until firm. It will require about one-half hour in a moderate oven.

Bain-marie. This is a term used in cookery for a vessel holding hot water in which another vessel may be heated at a temperature not above that of boiling water. Different dishes are variously allowed to stand, cook or bake in bain-marie. For example, Hollandaise sauce should be kept in bain-marie in hot water. Hollandaise or Béarnaise sauce, if kept in boiling water, would turn. A cream soup should be kept in boiling water, as extra cooking will not harm it. Timbale of chicken, custard for soup, or cup custard, should be cooked in bain-marie.

Purée Crécy (soup). Slice six carrots very thin, put in casserole with three ounces of butter, and simmer for thirty minutes. Then add three pints of well-seasoned chicken broth, and boil for one hour. Strain through a fine sieve. Serve in a separate dish small squares of bread fried in butter.

Roast leg of mutton. The leg of mutton should hang in the ice box at least four days before using. If too fresh it will be tough. Rub the mutton with salt and pepper and, if desired, a little garlic. Put in a roasting pan, one sliced onion, one sliced carrot, one bay leaf and two cloves. Now put in the mutton, with a piece of butter on top, and place in oven to roast. Baste continually. It will require from forty-five to sixty minutes to cook. If desired well done cook for another thirty minutes. When done take out the leg, drain off the fat, and make a gravy by adding one cup of stock and one spoonful of meat extract; boil, season, and strain.

JANUARY 27

BREAKFAST
  Stewed rhubarb
  Ham and eggs
  Rolls
  Coffee

LUNCHEON
  Salade thon mariné
  Stuffed breast of veal, au jus
  Asparagus tips, au gratin
  Potato salad
  Savarin au rhum
  Coffee

DINNER
  Potato and leek soup
  Corned beef and cabbage
  Plain boiled potatoes
  Broiled chicken on toast
  Lettuce with egg dressing
  Coupe St. Jacques
  Assorted cakes
  Coffee

Thon mariné salad. Tunny fish can be obtained in cans, the best quality being the French brands. Break up the fish with the fingers, and place on a platter with leaves of lettuce. The fish should be in pieces about one inch and a half thick. Sprinkle with salt, pepper, chopped parsley, chervil, and a little finely sliced chives, and a sauce of one-third vinegar and two-thirds olive oil.

Stuffed breast of veal, au jus. Have your butcher prepare a breast of veal ready for stuffing. Use the same dressing as for chicken, and sew up the end so the dressing will not fall out while roasting. Put in the roasting pan one sliced onion and one carrot. Put in the veal and sprinkle with salt and pepper. Put bits of butter all over the top and roast in oven, basting often. It will take about an hour to cook in a moderate oven. Remove the veal to platter when done, and make a sauce by adding to the gravy in pan one cup of bouillon and one spoonful of meat extract, boil for five minutes, and strain.

Asparagus tips, au gratin. Put the tips in a buttered pan or silver dish, cover with well-seasoned cream sauce, sprinkle with grated cheese and small bits of butter and bake in oven until brown.

Corned beef and cabbage. The best corned beef is that made from the brisket. Put on fire in cold water and skim when it comes to the boiling point. Cover and let it boil slowly until about three-quarters done. Then add two heads of well-washed cabbage cut in four, and cook with the beef for at least one hour.

JANUARY 28

BREAKFAST
- Farina with cream
- Omelet with fine herbs
- Rolls
- Coffee

LUNCHEON
- Grapefruit and orange en suprême
- Ripe olives
- Eggs Marigny
- Russian salad
- Caramel custard
- Coffee

DINNER
    Tomate Parisienne (cold)
    Consommé parfait
    Boiled salmon, Hollandaise
    Potatoes nature
    Fricandeau of veal, au jus
    Sorrel with eggs
    Carrots with cream
    Baba au rhum
    Coffee

Russian salad. Equal parts of boiled carrots, turnips, beets and potatoes, cut in small dice, boiled peas, boiled string beans cut in small pieces, and one slice of cold roast beef cut in small squares. Put all in salad bowl, season with salt, pepper, a little Cayenne pepper, and just enough tarragon vinegar to wet the mixture. Let stand for one hour, drain off the liquid, if any, and form the salad in pyramid shape in the bowl. Spread some thick mayonnaise over all, and garnish with boiled potatoes and truffles, cut like a five-cent piece, linking one to the other around the base of the salad like a chain. On top put a small flower of a boiled and seasoned cauliflower, and serve very cold.

Caramel custard. Put two ounces of sugar in a copper pan and cook until it is brown in color, then pour into a custard mould and allow to become cold. Mix four eggs with one-quarter of a pound of sugar, flavor with vanilla, add one pint of milk, and strain. Pour over the burned sugar, and fill the mould. Put in bain-marie and cook until firm. When cool, reverse the custard on a dish, and serve. The caramel at the bottom of the mould will serve as a sauce.

Tomate Parisienne (Hors d'oeuvres). Peel and slice four tomatoes and lay on platter with lettuce leaves. Cut the inside of a stalk of celery in very small dice, and six anchovies in small squares. Put in a bowl, add a pinch of salt, some fresh-ground black pepper, some chives, parsley and chervil chopped fine, and one spoonful of vinegar and two of olive oil. Mix well and pour over the tomatoes.

Sorrel. Sorrel is a fine vegetable for the promotion of health. Remove the stems from a peck of sorrel and wash the leaves in four different waters, to remove all the sand. Have a kettle with salted water on the fire. Put the sorrel into the boiling water and cook for ten minutes, stirring often. Pour off the water and let stand in the colander fifteen minutes so it will drain dry, then strain through a fine sieve. Then put the sorrel in a sauce pan with three ounces of butter and bring to the boiling point. Season with salt and pepper, and bind with two whole eggs, beaten. Do not let it boil after adding the eggs, but let it get just hot enough to give the sorrel a firm body. Garnish with the half of a hard boiled egg, if desired.

JANUARY 29

BREAKFAST
Orange juice
Boiled eggs
Rolls
Coffee

LUNCHEON
Hors d'oeuvres variés
Eggs à la Russe
Boiled beef tongue with spinach
Mashed potatoes
French pastry
Coffee

DINNER
Cream of canned peas
Sardines on toast
Roast beef au jus
Lima beans
Rissolées potatoes
Romaine salad
Raspberry Bavarois
Assorted cakes

Coffee

Eggs à la Russe. Spread a piece of toast with fresh caviar, put an egg fried in oil on top, and put anchovy sauce around the edge on the platter.

Eggs fried in oil. Fry the eggs one at a time. Have a very small frying pan with plenty of very hot olive oil in it. Drop a fresh egg in it, and turn with a wooden spoon. If any other kind of spoon is used the egg will stick to it. When of a good yellow color, take out and place on a towel, so the oil can drain off, and season with salt. The eggs should be soft inside, like a poached egg.

Anchovy sauce. To a cup of cream add one spoonful of essence of anchovies, or one teaspoonful of anchovy paste. Anchovy sauce is also made with sauce Allemande, white wine sauce, or even a brown sauce, if desired. The cream sauce with the essence is more commonly used with eggs.

Boiled beef tongue. Put a fresh beef tongue in cold water and bring to the boiling point, skim, add salt, one carrot, one onion, a bouquet garni, one stalk of celery, and one of leek. Boil until tongue is soft. The bouillon may be used for stock or soup, or to make caper sauce. For beef tongue with spinach, put plain boiled spinach on platter, sliced tongue on top, and pour a little of the broth over all.

Raspberry Bavarois. (For four or five persons.) One pint of milk, one pint of whipped cream, the yolks of four eggs, one-quarter pound of sugar, six sheets of French gelatine, and one-half pint of raspberry juice. Boil the milk with the sugar, then pour over the yolks, and set on the fire again until it thickens, but do not let it boil. Wash the gelatine in cold water, add to the mixture, and stir until melted. Then set aside until cold. Mix the raspberry pulp with the whipped cream, and stir into the mixture. Put in mould and place in ice box until set. Turn out on platter, and serve with whipped cream or raspberry syrup, separate or around the bavarois.

Sardines on toast. Take sardines from can and put on a fine thin wire broiler and heat quickly. Serve on toast with maître d'hôtel butter on top, and garnish with quartered lemons and parsley.

JANUARY 30

BREAKFAST
Baked apples with cream
Scrambled eggs with smoked beef
Rolls
English breakfast tea

LUNCHEON
Grapefruit with chestnuts
Consommé in cups
Deviled crab
Lemon pie
Coffee

DINNER
Toke Point oysters
Potage tapioca, Crécy
Terrapin, Maryland
Squab chicken, Michels
Stewed tomatoes
Cèpes Tyrolienne (cold)
Fancy ice cream
Cakes
Coffee

Grapefruit with chestnuts. Cut a grapefruit in two and cut free the sections with a pointed knife. Pour a little maraschino in the center, and place a marron glacé (candied chestnut) on top.

Deviled crabs. Simmer the flakes of two crabs and one-half of a chopped onion in butter. Season with salt and Cayenne pepper, add two cups of thick cream sauce, one dash of Worcestershire sauce, one spoonful of English mustard, and a little chopped chives. Bring to a boil, and bind with the yolks of two eggs. Then fill the crab shells, spread a little French mustard over the top, sprinkle with bread crumbs, place a small piece of butter on each, and bake in the oven. When brown serve on napkin with lemon and parsley.

Potage tapioca, Crécy. Half consommé tapioca and half potage Crécy, mixed. No croûtons.

Stewed tomatoes. Peel six tomatoes, and cut in four. Squeeze out half of the juice, and put the tomatoes in a vessel with three ounces of butter, season with salt, pepper and a pinch of powdered sugar, cover, and simmer until done.

Cèpes Tyrolienne (cold). Cut in small dices one carrot and one celery root, and put in casserole with one chopped onion and two ounces of butter. Simmer. Then add one glass of white wine and reduce. Then add one-half cup of tomato sauce, some chopped chervil, and one can of sliced cèpes. Serve cold.

Squab chicken à la Michels. Season four squab chickens well with salt and pepper, both inside and out. Put in iron pot with a quarter of a pound of sweet butter and one onion cut in two. Put the pot on the fire and simmer slowly, until the chicken and onion are of a good yellow color, turning them often while cooking. Then add one tablespoonful of white wine and one of chicken broth, cover, and put in oven for ten minutes, basting frequently. Put the chickens on a platter, take out the onion, and boil the sauce remaining in pot with the addition of one teaspoonful of meat extract. Strain over the chicken.

JANUARY 31

BREAKFAST

Oatmeal with cream

Calf's liver and bacon

Rolls

Coffee

LUNCHEON

Oysters Kirkpatrick

Country sausages with baked apples

Potato salad

Cabinet pudding

Coffee

DINNER

        Potage Windsor
        Green olives
        Fillet of sole, Admiral
        Saddle of lamb, mint sauce
        String beans
        Potato croquettes
        Hearts of lettuce
        Pineapple biscuit glacé
        Assorted cakes
        Coffee

Oysters Kirkpatrick. Season some oysters on half shell with salt, pepper and a little Worcestershire sauce, cover with tomato ketchup, sprinkle with grated cheese, put a small piece of butter on top of each, and bake in their own shells for five minutes. Serve quartered lemon separate.

Cabinet pudding. Fill a well-buttered pudding mould with left-over pieces of sponge, layer or other kinds of cake, cut in small squares, and mix with one-quarter pound of seedless raisins. Then make a custard of three eggs, one-quarter pound of sugar, one pint of milk and a little vanilla flavoring. Mix well, strain, and pour over the cake in the moulds, and bake in bain-marie for about forty minutes. Remove from the mould and serve hot, with vanilla cream sauce.

Fillet of sole, Admiral. Put fillets of sole in a buttered sauté pan, decorate the top with fish force meat in the shape of an anchor, and cook in white wine. When done serve with a white wine sauce, with shrimps, oysters and clams cut in small pieces, in it. Garnish with fleurons.

Potage Windsor. Put in roasting pan five pounds of veal bones, one carrot and one onion sliced, a piece of leek, a piece of celery, a bouquet garni, and three ounces of butter. Roast in oven until well browned, then transfer to a pot and add one gallon of water, six calf's feet and a little salt, and boil until the feet are cooked. Strain the broth. Allow the feet to cool, remove the meat from the bones, and slice in very thin strips. Now put four ounces of butter in a vessel, heat, and add four ounces of flour and cook until golden brown. Then add two quarts of the broth, and boil for thirty minutes. Strain, add the calf's feet, one carrot boiled and cut in very thin round slices, some small chicken dumplings, a few French peas, and one-half cup of sherry wine. Season with salt and Cayenne pepper.

FEBRUARY 1

BREAKFAST
  Fried hominy
  Currant jelly
  Crescents
  Coffee

LUNCHEON
  Poached eggs with clams, Créole
  Chicken croquettes with peas
  Camembert cheese and crackers
  Coffee

DINNER
  Oxtail soup, English style
  Boiled brook trout, Hollandaise
  Potatoes nature
  Roast stuffed duckling, apple sauce
  Broiled sweet potatoes
  Brussels sprouts in bouillon
  Romaine salad
  French pancake
  Coffee

Clams, Créole. Heat two dozen clams in their own juice, but do not allow them to boil. Then add one pint of Créole sauce.

Poached eggs with clams, Créole. Serve poached eggs on toast, covered with clams Créole.

Ox tail, English style. Cut two ox tails in small pieces, put on the fire in cold water, salt, and bring to the boiling point. Take off the stove and allow to cool. Put in sauce pan four ounces of butter, melt, add the oxtail, and roast until colored. Then sprinkle the pieces with two large spoonsful of flour, and cook again until of a good brown color. Then add one gallon of bouillon, stock or hot water; bring to a boil, and skim. Then boil for one hour. Now add three carrots and two turnips cut in very small squares, and one pound of whole barley, and boil for two hours. Then add one pint of purée of tomatoes, one spoonful of Worcestershire sauce, salt, pepper, a little Cayenne, some chopped parsley, and one-half cup of tomato ketchup. Boil again for ten minutes, and before serving add one glass of sherry wine.

Broiled sweet potatoes. Peel four boiled sweet potatoes, and slice lengthwise, one-quarter inch in thickness. Sprinkle with salt, wet with olive oil, and broil on both sides on an iron broiler. Serve on a platter with melted butter poured over them.

Brussels sprouts in bouillon. Clean and wash thoroughly one quart of Brussels sprouts. Put a vessel on the fire, with one gallon of water and a tablespoonful of salt. When boiling add the sprouts and cook for five minutes; then cool off with cold water. Put the cold sprouts in a casserole, add two ounces of butter, salt, pepper, one cup of bouillon and a little chopped parsley. Cover, and simmer until well done. Sprouts should be served whole, so do not touch with spoon while cooking.

FEBRUARY 2

BREAKFAST
  Stewed rhubarb
  Boiled eggs
  Dry toast
  Coffee

LUNCHEON
  Smoked goosebreast
  Tomcods, meunière
  Broiled fresh spareribs, with lentils
  Vanilla bavarois, with Bar le Duc
  Cookies

Demi tasse

DINNER

Consommé Doria

Scallops, Jerusalem

Spring lamb tenderloin, Thomas

Fried egg plant

Chicory and escarole salad

Homemade apple pudding

Coffee

Tomcods, meunière. Season six tomcods with salt and pepper, and roll in flour. Melt four ounces of butter in a frying pan, put in the tomcods and fry. When done put on platter and sprinkle with chopped parsley and the juice of two lemons. Put four ounces of butter in the pan and cook to the color of a hazelnut. Pour the butter over the fish, garnish with quartered lemon and parsley in branches.

Broiled spareribs with lentils. Broil some spareribs and place on platter. Garnish with lentils, and serve with a border of Madeira sauce.

Lentils. Soak two pounds of lentils in cold water for six hours, then put on fire with one quart of water, a pinch of salt, one ham bone, one carrot, one onion and a bouquet garni. Boil for about two hours, when the lentils should be soft; remove the vegetables and the bouquet, and drain off the water. Then chop two large onions very fine, put in casserole with three ounces of butter, cover, and simmer until done. Add the lentils and a cup of brown meat gravy, some chopped parsley and ground pepper, simmer for twenty minutes, and serve hot.

Lentil salad. Take some of the boiled lentils, before the onions and brown gravy have been added, and serve with French dressing.

Vanilla Bavarois with Bar le Duc. Bar le Duc is a currant jelly made in the village of Bar le Duc, France. There are two kinds, red and white. Make a vanilla bavarois, place on platter, and pour some red Bar le Duc around the base.

Homemade cookies. Work one-quarter pound of butter and one-quarter pound of sugar together until creamy, then add three eggs, one by one, and whip well. Then add one-quarter pound of sifted flour and some flavoring, preferably the rind of a lemon. Dress the batter in fancy, or plain round, shapes, on a buttered pan, and bake in a quick oven.

FEBRUARY 3

BREAKFAST
 Grapefruit
 Ham and eggs
 Rolls
 Coffee

LUNCHEON
 Canapé of sardines
 Eggs Benedict
 Sweetbread cutlets, cream sauce
 Broiled fresh mushrooms
 Fruit salad, Chantilly
 Coffee

DINNER
 Potage Lamballe
 Frogs' legs, sauté à sec
 Wiener schnitzel
 Spaghetti Milanaise
 Terrine de foie gras, cold
 Lettuce salad
 Nesselrode pudding
 Cakes
 Coffee

Eggs Benedict. Cut an English muffin in two, toast, and put on platter. Put a slice of broiled ham on top of each half, a poached egg on top of the ham, cover all with Hollandaise, and lay a slice of truffle on top of the sauce.

Wiener Schnitzel. Cut from a leg of veal some cutlets; or have your butcher cut them for you. Season with salt and pepper, roll in flour, then in beaten eggs, and then in bread crumbs. Put some melted butter in a frying pan and fry the cutlets, or schnitzel, on both sides, until yellow and well done. Dish up on a platter with tomato sauce. Put on each schnitzel a thin slice of lemon. Roll a fillet of anchovy around your finger to form a ring, place on a slice of lemon and fill the ring with capers.

Fruit salad, Chantilly. Slice some fresh fruit, such as oranges, pears, pineapple, apples, strawberries, cherries, etc. Put in a bowl, add one spoonful of granulated sugar, one pony of kirschwasser or maraschino, and allow to macerate for about an hour. Put in glasses or saucers, and serve with whipped cream on top.

Fruit salad au kirsch. Same as above, but use kirschwasser only, to macerate, and omit the whipped cream.

Fruit salad au marasquin. Same as au kirsch, only use maraschino instead of kirschwasser.

FEBRUARY 4

BREAKFAST
  Guava jelly
  Rolled oats with cream
  Plain omelet
  Rolls
  Coffee

LUNCHEON
  Hors d'oeuvres variés
  Fillet of halibut, au vin blanc
  Broiled pig's feet, special
  Celery root, field and beet salad
  Assorted fruit
  Coffee

DINNER
  Bisque of clams

                    Broiled Alaska black cod
                    Breast of squab under glass, St. Francis
                    Asparagus Polonaise
                    Coupe Viviane
                    Assorted cakes
                    Coffee

Broiled Alaska black cod. This Alaskan fish is brought from the north frozen, and is very fine, being rich and fat. Broiling is the best way of preparing it, as it needs a quick fire to cook the oil in the fish. Season well, and serve with maître d'hôtel sauce made with plenty of lemon juice.

Asparagus Polonaise. Put four pounds of boiled fresh, or two cans, of asparagus on a platter. Have the asparagus very hot. Sprinkle the tips with salt and pepper, one chopped boiled egg, and some chopped parsley. Melt in a pan, three ounces of sweet butter, add two tablespoonsful of bread crumbs, fry until brown, and pour over the tips of the asparagus.

Breast of squab under glass, St. Francis. Season the breast of a raw squab with salt and pepper, and roll in flour. Fry in butter for two minutes, or until nice and brown. Fry in the same butter, very lightly, one slice of Virginia ham. Then fry in same pan the heads of four fresh mushrooms, well seasoned. Put a slice of toast in a buttered shirred egg dish, put the ham on the toast, the breast of squab on the ham, and the mushrooms on top. Pour well-seasoned cream sauce over all, cover with a glass bell that fits just inside of the edge of the shirred egg dish, put in the oven and cook for ten minutes.

Boiled lettuce. Boil six heads of lettuce in salted water. When done strain off the water and pound the lettuce through a fine colander. Add two ounces of butter and one cup of cream, heat well, and serve.

FEBRUARY 5

BREAKFAST
  Baked apples with cream
  Buttered toast
  Cocoa

LUNCHEON
  Omelet with soft clams, Newburg
  Breaded lamb chops, tomato sauce
  New string beans
  Potatoes au gratin
  Mince pie
  Coffee

DINNER
  Seapuit oysters
  Potage Talleyrand
  Planked smelts
  Tournedos Rossini
  Jets de houblons
  Gauffrette potatoes
  Romaine salad, Roquefort dressing
  Curaçao sorbet
  Alsatian wafers
  Demi tasse

Sauce Newburg. Put in a vessel one cup of well-seasoned cream sauce, one cup of thick cream and one gill of sherry wine. Bring to the boiling point and bind with the yolk of one egg and a little cream. Then stir slowly into the sauce two tablespoonsful of lobster or crayfish butter. This sauce is used a great deal in hotel and restaurant cookery.

Soft clams, Newburg. Take the bellies of two dozen soft clams and put in a buttered sauté pan, add one spoonful of Madeira wine, cover the pan, and warm them through. Do not stir, as the clams will break easily. Then add one and one-half cups of sauce Newburg, well seasoned with salt, pepper and a little Cayenne pepper. Mix and serve in a chafing dish.

Omelet with soft clams. Make a plain well-seasoned omelet. Put at each end a bouquet of clams Newburg, and pour on each side of the omelet a little sauce Newburg.

Potage Talleyrand. Put in soup tureen one quart of consommé tapioca, one grated fresh, or two grated canned truffles, one glass of dry sherry wine, a pinch of Cayenne pepper.

Tournedos. Tournedos are small tenderloin beef steaks, trimmed free of fat. They may be either broiled or sautéed, and served with maître d'hôtel sauce. Mostly used as an entrée with fancy garniture.

Tournedos Rossini. Salt and pepper the tournedos, sauté in butter, and put on a platter. Take one slice of fresh goose liver (or Strassbourg goose liver au natural), season, roll in flour, sauté in butter, and put on top of the tournedo. Simmer a large head of fresh mushroom in butter, and place on top of the goose liver, lay two slices of truffle on top of the mushroom, and pour well-seasoned Madeira sauce over all.

FEBRUARY 6

BREAKFAST
  Preserved figs
  Scrambled eggs with bacon
  Rolls
  Coffee

LUNCHEON
  Antipasto
  Essence of chicken in cups
  Cheese straws
  Bear steak, port wine sauce
  Chestnuts and prunes
  Fried egg plant
  Mexican salad
  Corn meal pudding

       Coffee
      DINNER
       Clam chowder
       Ripe olives
       Striped bass sauté, miller style
       O'Brien potatoes
       Asparagus Hollandaise
       Cold Westphalia ham
       Omelette soufflée à la vanille
       Coffee

Scrambled eggs with bacon (1). Put some plain scrambled eggs in a deep platter with strips of broiled bacon over the eggs.

(2) Cut six slices of bacon in small squares, put in casserole with one-half ounce of butter and fry slowly until crisp. Add ten beaten eggs mixed with one-half cup of cream, season with salt and pepper, and cook in the usual manner.

Antipasto. This is an Italian relish (hors d'oeuvre), and can be obtained in cans. It consists of tunny fish, sardines, pickles, capers, etc., preserved in oil. Serve on a napkin, in the can, with quartered lemons and parsley around the sides.

Essence of chicken. Put in a casserole one chopped raw fowl, or plenty of carcasses, necks, etc., of raw chickens. Add the whites of three eggs, stir well, and add slowly two quarts of strong chicken broth. Bring to a boil, strain through a napkin, and serve in cups.

O'Brien potatoes. Peel two large boiled potatoes, cut in one-half inch squares, and put in hot fat to gain color. Cut two red peppers (pimentos) in small squares and put in a sauté pan with one ounce of butter. When the peppers are hot add the potatoes, season with salt and pepper, and mix carefully so the potatoes will not break.

Omelette Soufflée. Mix one-half pound of sugar with the yolks of two eggs, add one-half of a split vanilla bean, and beat until light and fluffy.

Remove the pieces of vanilla bean. Beat the whites of eight eggs until absolutely stiff, and then add to the batter lightly. Arrange on a silver platter in fancy shape, and decorate with a pastry bag with a fine tube. Dust with powdered sugar, and bake in a rather hot oven for a few minutes.

FEBRUARY 7

BREAKFAST
  Cactus fruit with lemon
  Broiled pigs' feet, Chili sauce
  Shirred eggs with parsley
  Dry toast
  Cocoa

LUNCHEON
  Eggs Lackmée
  Lamb steak, Bercy
  String beans
  Mashed potatoes
  Fruit salad au Marasquin
  Coffee

DINNER
  Consommé Julienne
  Fillet of flounder, Cansale
  Tenderloin of beef, Malvina
  Escarole and chicory salad
  Almond cake
  Coffee

Cactus fruit with lemon. Slice some cactus fruit and serve on ice, with powdered sugar and lemon separate. No cream.

Broiled pigs' feet, Chili sauce. Split some cooked pigs' feet, season, roll in bread crumbs, sprinkle with oil and broil. Put on platter and garnish with lemon and parsley. Serve hot or cold Chili sauce, separate.

Shirred eggs with parsley. Crack two eggs on a buttered shirred egg dish, season with salt and pepper, sprinkle with fresh-chopped parsley, and bake in oven for three minutes.

Eggs Lackmée. Put four poached eggs on toast. Chop some boiled chicken very fine, add one cup of cream sauce, one-half cup of cream, put on the stove and bring to the boiling point, season with salt and a little Cayenne pepper, and pour over the eggs.

Lamb steak. Cut the steak crosswise from a leg of young lamb, and about one inch in thickness. Season with salt and pepper, roll in oil and broil; or sauté in pan with butter. Use as an entrée dish, or in place of the roast.

Garniture Bercy. Bercy is used with steaks, chops, fish, etc. Prepare as follows: Mix one-quarter pound of fresh butter with salt, pepper, three fine chopped shallots, one small piece of garlic mashed fine, some chopped parsley, chervil and chives. Spread over the meats or fish, and put in hot oven for two minutes. (Called also sauce Bercy.)

Fillet of flounder, Cansale. Put four fillets of flounder in a buttered pan, season with salt and pepper, add the juice of one dozen oysters, one-half wineglass full of white wine, cover with buttered paper, and bake in oven. When done remove the fillets and add to the pan one-half pint of white wine sauce, and boil for ten minutes. Bind with the yolk of one egg, and strain. Poach the dozen oysters, and, with a small can of French mushrooms, add to the sauce, and pour over the fish.

Tenderloin of beef, Malvina. A roast tenderloin with sauce Madère, garnished with small onions sauté, potatoes rissolées, and whole chestnuts glacé au Madère.

Chestnuts glacé. Put one-half pound of boiled chestnuts in a sauté pan with two spoonsful of meat extract, and cook for ten minutes.

Chestnuts glacé au Madère. Add to chestnuts glacé a little sauce Madère, just before serving.

FEBRUARY 8

BREAKFAST
  Baked apples with cream
  Boiled eggs
  Dry toast
  Chocolate with whipped cream

LUNCHEON
  Omelette Louis XIV
  Chickens' livers sauté, au Madère
  Purée of Lima beans
  Sago pudding
  Coffee

DINNER
  Seapuit oysters
  Cream of celery, Kalamazoo
  Ripe California olives
  Fillet of pompano, en papillote
  Roast chicken
  Watercress salad
  Château potatoes
  Fresh asparagus, Hollandaise
  Peach Mona Lisa
  Assorted cakes
  Coffee

Omelette Louis XIV. Chop the white meat of a boiled fowl very fine, mix with one truffle cut in small dices and one-half cup of well-seasoned cream sauce. Place in the center of a plain omelet, turn on a platter, and pour some cream sauce around the edge.

Chickens' livers sauté, Forestière. Clean a dozen chicken livers, cut in two, and season with salt and pepper. Melt a piece of butter in frying pan, add the livers, and sauté over a quick fire for a few minutes. Slice one pound of fresh mushrooms and fry them in butter. Then put the mushrooms and livers together in a sauce pot on the stove, and cover with two cupsful of brown gravy or Madeira sauce. Get as hot as possible without boiling, serve in deep dish, or chafing dish, with chopped parsley on top.

Purée of Lima beans. Take one can, or a pound of fresh boiled Lima beans, and pass through a fine sieve. Put in pot, add two ounces of butter, season with salt and pepper, and serve hot. If too thick add a soupspoonful of cream or consommé.

Cream of celery, Kalamazoo. Make a cream of celery soup. Take the inside of two stalks of celery and cut in very small dices boiled, and use for garnishing.

Fillet of pompano en papillote. Take four small Pacific pompano, or the fillets of a large Florida pompano, season, roll in flour, and put in pan in two ounces of hot butter. Fry on both sides until nearly done. Simmer two chopped shallots in one ounce of butter for a minute, then add six chopped fresh mushrooms, and simmer for ten minutes. Now add one spoonful of Madeira sauce, season with salt and pepper, and cook for five minutes to a purée. Add the juice of a lemon, some chopped parsley, and one ounce of sweet butter. Now cut four pieces of manilla paper in the shape of a heart about ten inches high and fourteen inches wide. Fold in center, then open out flat on the table and oil well on one side. Put a teaspoonful of the mushroom purée on one half of the paper, place the pompano on top, and another spoonful of the purée on top of the fish. Now fold the free side of the paper over the top, and turn in the edges to close tight the opening. Put on a flat pan and place in an oven for a few minutes. Be careful not to burn, and serve in the papers on a silver platter. Other fish may be substituted for pompano if desired.

Papillote, club style (for fish). Fry the fish as above. Omit the purée of mushrooms and use, instead, a piece of butter, a slice of fresh-boiled hot potato, and one slice of lime. Finish as above.

Veal chops en papillote. Season four veal chops with salt and pepper, fry in butter, and finish in paper, with the purée of mushrooms and the addition of a slice of cooked ham on top, before folding the paper.

FEBRUARY 9

BREAKFAST
  Stewed prunes
  Broiled salt mackerel, melted butter
  Baked potatoes
  Rolls
  Coffee

LUNCHEON
  Eggs Henri IV
  Pork tenderloin, sauce Madère
  Fried sweet potatoes
  Stewed apples
  Sherry wine jelly
  Coffee

DINNER
  Consommé national
  Radishes
  Fried fillet of sole, Maréchal
  Roast rack of lamb, mint sauce
  String beans
  Mashed potatoes
  Nesselrode pudding
  Cakes
  Coffee

Wine jelly. Dissolve four ounces of French gelatine in two quarts of water, add one pound of sugar, the rind and juice of six lemons, the juice of three oranges, a piece of cinnamon stick, and six cloves. Stir well and put on fire to boil. Then stir quickly into the jelly the whites of six eggs, partly beaten, and boil again. Then take off the fire and strain through a flannel jelly bag, and add the flavoring desired. Pour into jelly moulds and put on ice until firm. To remove the jelly, dip the moulds in hot water, and turn out on a cold dish. For the following jellies use a wine glassful of the respective wines or liqueurs for flavoring: Sherry wine, maraschino, Rhein wine, claret, port wine, anisette, kirschwasser, champagne, Burgundy, Moselle wine, Chartreuse, brandy, Bénédictine, Cognac, fine champagne, etc.

Fruit jelly. Cut or slice all kinds of fresh fruit in season, put in jelly mould and cover with wine jelly. Put in ice box until firm.

Jelly à la Russe. Put some empty jelly moulds on ice until cold, then pour a little wine jelly in the bottom and allow to set. Do not let the balance of the jelly set, but add a pony of Russian kümmel, put in bowl and beat with a whip until it looks like white frost. Then fill the moulds to the top with the beaten jelly, and set in the ice box until needed.

Fillet of sole, Maréchal. Salt and pepper the fillets, dip in milk, then in flour, then in beaten eggs, and finally in bread crumbs. Fry in swimming lard, and serve on napkin with lemon and fried parsley. Serve the following sauce separate: Two cups of cream sauce, one dozen parboiled oysters, one-quarter pound of picked shrimps, and six sliced canned mushrooms.

FEBRUARY 10

BREAKFAST
- Grapefruit
- Omelet with chives
- Corn muffins
- Coffee

LUNCHEON
- Pickled oysters
- Toasted rye bread
- Consommé vermicelli
- Calf's head à la poulette
- Potato croquettes
- Hot mince pie
- American cheese
- Coffee

DINNER
- Purée of pheasant, St. Hubert
- Planked smelts
- Bacon and cabbage
- Boiled potatoes
- Roast ribs of beef, au jus
- Chiffonnade salad

Tutti frutti ice cream
Assorted cakes
Coffee

Consommé vermicelli. Boil one-half pound of vermicelli in two quarts of salt water for five minutes. Drain, and add to three pints of consommé. Serve grated cheese separate.

Calf's head, poulette. Take one boiled calf's head and cut in pieces two inches square. Mix with one quart of poulette sauce, and serve in chafing dish.

Purée of pheasant, St. Hubert. Remove the breast of a roasted pheasant and cut in small squares. Put the rest of the pheasant in a pot and cover with two quarts of bouillon, add a bouquet garni, and boil for one hour. In a sauce pot put three ounces of butter; when hot add three spoonsful of flour, and allow to become nice and brown. Then strain the broth into the sauce pot and boil for thirty minutes. Chop the pheasant very fine and add to the soup, boil again, and strain through a fine sieve. Season with salt and pepper, add the cut-up pheasant breast, and a glass of fine dry sherry wine.

Bacon and cabbage. Cut a large head of cabbage in four, wash well, and put in two quarts of water, with a little salt, and boil. Then drain off the water, add fresh water and two pounds of bacon, and boil until the bacon is well done. Put the cabbage on a platter, slice the bacon and put on top of the cabbage.

Tutti frutti ice cream. Macerate one-quarter of a pound of chopped candied mixed fruit in a pony of maraschino. Mix thoroughly with one quart of vanilla ice cream. Put in the bottom of a mould a little raspberry water ice, and fill to the top with the ice cream and fruit. Pack in ice and rock salt, and leave for about an hour and a half. Turn out on platter and decorate with candied cherries and angelica.

FEBRUARY 11

BREAKFAST
  Oatmeal with cream
  Rolls
  Chocolate
  Whipped cream

LUNCHEON
  Eggs Brésilienne
  Sirloin steak, marchand de vin
  Fried egg plant
  Farina pudding
  Coffee

DINNER
  Potage Waldaise
  Fish dumplings, white wine sauce
  Mutton chops, provençale
  Mashed potatoes
  String beans
  Hearts of romaine
  Fancy ice cream
  Cakes   Coffee

Eggs Brésilienne. Put some boiled rice on a platter, place a poached egg on top, and cover with tomato sauce mixed with a little chopped ham.

Sirloin steak, marchand de vin. Cut four slices of sirloin steak about one-half inch thick, season with salt and pepper, and roll in flour. Have three ounces of hot butter in a pan and fry the steaks for two minutes. Remove the steaks to platter. Chop two shallots very fine and put in pan, allow to become hot, add one-half glass of claret, and reduce one-half. Then add one spoonful of meat extract, the juice of one lemon, and some chopped parsley and pour over the steaks. Garnish with Parisian potatoes.

Parisian potatoes. Take some large potatoes and cut out a quart of small potatoes with a round Parisian spoon. Put on fire in cold water, with one spoonful of salt, and boil for three minutes. Drain off the water and put the potatoes in a flat sauté pan with three ounces of butter. Put in oven and roast for about twelve minutes, or until golden yellow. Try with fingers to see if done. Serve in a deep dish.

Potage Waldaise. Mix one quart of consommé tapioca with one quart of purée of tomato soup, add four slices of boiled ham cut in small squares.

Fish dumplings, white wine sauce. Remove the skin and bones from one pound of halibut, sole, salmon or other fish, put in mortar, mash well, and mix with the following dough: One cup of boiling water, one ounce of butter, and one-half cup of flour, well mixed. Let cool, stir in the yolks of two eggs, and mix with the mashed fish. Season with salt and a little Cayenne pepper, strain through a fine sieve, place in a pan on ice, and stir in slowly one-quarter pint of thick cream, adding it little by little. To make dumplings, drop teaspoonful of this forcemeat, or stuffing, into boiling fish broth, bouillon, or water with salt, and cook very slowly for five minutes. Serve in chafing dish covered with white wine sauce. These dumplings are also called quenelles of fish, and are used for fish patties, vol au vent, or garniture for fish. If made very small, can be served with clam broth. The forcemeat can be used for fish timbales and stuffing for fish.

Timbale of bass. Make a force meat as above, with any kind of bass, fill small well-buttered timbale moulds, and boil in bain-marie. Then cover with buttered paper and put in oven for ten minutes. Turn out on platter, and serve with any kind of fish sauce. For a fancy decoration slices of truffles or pimentos may be cut in the shape of stars, crescents, initials, etc., and placed in the bottom of the timbale moulds, then fill with the forcemeat and cook.

FEBRUARY 12

BREAKFAST
Sliced pineapple
Broiled lamb kidneys with bacon
Lyonnaise potatoes

LUNCHEON
Eggs à la tripe
Kingfish sauté meunière
Cucumber salad

Rolls
Coffee

Chicken sauté, Parisienne
French peas
Corn meal pudding
Coffee

DINNER

Potage Minestra
Queen olives
Fillet of barbel, régence
Tournedos Beresford
Potatoes château
Asparagus Hollandaise
Baked Alaska
Coffee

Eggs à la tripe. Slice an onion very fine, put in casserole with two ounces of butter, cover, and simmer. Cook until the onions are soft, but not colored. Then add two spoonsful of flour, allow to get hot, pour in one pint of boiling milk, season with salt and pepper, and boil for five minutes. Slice eight hard-boiled eggs about one-quarter inch in thickness, put in the sauce and cook until hot. Serve in chafing dish, or deep dish, with chopped parsley on top.

Chicken sauté, Parisienne (1). Joint a young chicken and sauté in pan with two ounces of butter. Season with salt and pepper, and when done add two cups of tomato sauce and one dozen sliced canned French mushrooms. Cook for two minutes in the sauce, dress the chicken on platter, pour the sauce over it, and garnish with macaroni in cream.

(2) Joint the chicken and put in sauté pan with two ounces of butter, and season with salt and pepper. When nearly done, add two chopped shallots and heat them through, only. Add one cup of sauce Madère, the juice of one lemon, and some chopped parsley. Serve with Parisian potatoes.

Sago pudding. One quart of milk, one-half of a split vanilla bean, one-quarter pound of sago, six ounces of sugar, the yolks of six eggs and the whites of six eggs. Boil the milk and the vanilla bean together, add the sago, and cook until well done and like a stiff batter. Take off the fire, add the sugar and the yolks, and mix well. Beat the whites until very stiff and dry, and then add to the batter and mix lightly. Put in buttered moulds and bake in moderate oven for nearly an hour. Turn out of moulds and serve with vanilla sauce.

Corn meal, rice, tapioca and farina puddings are made in the same manner as sago pudding.

Sago pudding, family style. One quart of milk, one-half of a split vanilla bean, three ounces of sago, six ounces of sugar, two eggs and one cup of cream. Boil the milk with the vanilla bean (or one-half teaspoonful of vanilla extract), add the sago, and cook well. Mix the sugar, eggs and cream, and add to the milk and sago. Pour in pudding dishes or bowl, put in hot oven to color the top, and serve either hot or cold, with cream separate.

Rice, corn meal, tapioca, farina or vermicelli puddings, family style, are made in the same manner as sago pudding, family style.

FEBRUARY 13

BREAKFAST
 Stewed prunes
 Boiled eggs
 Buttered toast
 Cocoa with whipped cream

LUNCHEON
 Eggs Troubadour
 Haricot of mutton
 French pastry
 Coffee

DINNER
 Potage Voisin
 Smoked goosebreast
 Fillet of sole, Choisy

Sweetbreads Eugénie
Roast leg of lamb, au jus
Julienne potatoes
Celery mayonnaise
Curaçao jelly
Coffee

Eggs Troubadour. Spread four pieces of toast with purée de foie gras (goose liver pâté), put a poached egg on top of each, and cover with sauce Périgord.

Haricot of mutton (stew). Cut five pounds of lean shoulder of mutton in pieces two inches square. Put in roasting pan with a little butter or fat, season with salt and pepper, and roast in oven until nice and brown. Add four spoonsful of flour and roast again until the flour is brown. Then put in a casserole and cover with boiling water, add a bouquet garni, six French carrots, six turnips cut in small pieces, season with salt and pepper, and boil for one hour. Remove the bouquet garni, and add one pint of purée of tomatoes, or a can of tomatoes strained through a fine sieve, and boil again, with the pot covered, until done. Before serving add some boiled string beans and chopped parsley. A little Worcestershire sauce may be added if desired.

French pastry. This is a term used in hotels and restaurants for a platter of mixed individual fancy cakes, such as éclairs, fruit tartelettes, moka cake, Napoleons, apple turnovers, Pont Neuf cakes, jalousie, cream puffs, etc.

Potage Voisin. Half purée of peas and half purée Crécy. Before serving add a handful of boiled rice.

Smoked goosebreast (Hors d'oeuvre). The most common goosebreast is imported from Germany; that made in the United States is seldom to be found in the markets. Do not cook; slice very thin, and serve on an ice-cold china platter, decorated with chopped meat jelly, and garnished with parsley in branches.

Fillet of sole, Choisy. Put the four fillets of a sole in a buttered pan, season with salt and a little Cayenne pepper, add one-half glass of white wine, cover with a buttered paper, and bake in oven. When done dress on a platter, and cover with green Hollandaise sauce, with a slice of truffle on top.

Green coloring (Vert d'épinards). Mash in mortar a peck of well-washed spinach. When very fine strain through a piece of cheesecloth, put in a bowl, set in hot water (bain-marie), and boil until set. When cold it will be a firm green mass, and may be used for coloring sauces, soups, etc.

Green Hollandaise sauce. Mix one pint of Hollandaise sauce with one spoonful of green coloring (Vert d'épinards).

FEBRUARY 14

BREAKFAST
　Stewed rhubarb
　Plain omelet
　Rolls
　Coffee

LUNCHEON
　Smoked eels
　Pumpernickel with sweet butter
　Roast loin of pork with sauerkraut
　Plain boiled potatoes
　German huckleberry pie
　Coffee

DINNER
　Lynn Haven oysters
　Cream of cauliflower
　Pickles
　Broiled Spanish mackerel, sauce fleurette
　Chicken sauté, Portugaise
　Artichokes Hollandaise
　Hearts of lettuce, French dressing
　Diplomate pudding

Assorted cakes
Coffee

Smoked eels. Imported German canned eels. Serve on napkin with quartered lemons and parsley in branches.

Sauerkraut, Alsatian style. Spread one-quarter of a pound of goose grease (lard will do) in the bottom of a casserole, then put in one pound of sauerkraut, then two pounds of bacon, then another pound of sauerkraut, and another quarter pound of goose grease on top. Then add a pint of white wine and a pint of bouillon, cover with a buttered paper and the casserole cover, put on the stove and bring to a boil. Then put in oven and cook for an hour and a half. Serve the sauerkraut on a platter, with the bacon sliced, as a garnish.

Sauerkraut, German style. Put one-quarter pound of lard in a casserole, add one pound of sauerkraut, two pounds of salt pork, one bouquet garni, one whole onion, one carrot, and on top another pound of sauerkraut. Then add one glass of vinegar, two spoonsful of sugar, and one pint of bouillon. Cover, and cook in oven for two hours. Then remove the bouquet garni, onion and carrot, and serve the sauerkraut with the salt pork.

Sauerkraut, Hungarian style. Put in a casserole one-quarter pound of lard and one pound of sauerkraut. Sprinkle on top one spoonful of paprika and three peeled and chopped tomatoes. Then add two pounds of bacon and another pound of sauerkraut, and sprinkle again with another spoonful of paprika and three chopped tomatoes. Add a pint of sweet white wine and a pint of bouillon, and one bouquet garni. Cover and bake in oven for one hour and a half. Remove the bouquet garni, and serve with the bacon sliced.

Special notice for sauerkraut. Avoid salt, as the sauerkraut is seasoned, and the bacon and salt pork are salty also. If the raw sauerkraut is too salty, lay it in a dish pan, cover with water, and squeeze out with the hands immediately. Do not let it remain in the water but a second.

Other meats may be cooked in the sauerkraut, as beef and pork together, lamb and pork, beef and lamb, or pheasant or other game.

FEBRUARY 15

BREAKFAST
- Baked apples with cream
- Baked beans, Boston style
- Boston brown bread
- Coffee

LUNCHEON
- Eggs Bagration
- Chicken hash on toast
- Chocolate éclairs
- Coffee

DINNER
- Hors d'oeuvres variés
- Mock turtle soup
- Ripe California olives
- Aiguillettes of sole, hotelière
- Sweetbreads braisé, Clamart
- Roast partridge, bread sauce
- Jets de houblons
- Soufflée potatoes
- Endives salad
- Fancy ice cream
- Assorted cakes
- Coffee

Eggs Bagration. Put on a platter some boiled rice, lay a fresh hard-boiled egg, cut in two, on top, and cover with the following sauce. Take any kind of cold meats that may be left over, such as lamb, beef, ham or tongue, and cut in small dices. Also a few mushrooms and truffles cut in the same way. Put in a casserole with a cup of cream sauce, season with salt and pepper, and bring to a boil.

Chicken hash on toast. Cut the breast of a boiled fowl in small squares. Put in a casserole one cup of cream sauce, one gill of thick cream and the chicken, season with salt and pepper, and cook together. Serve on a platter on dry toast.

Aiguillettes of sole, hotelière. Put aiguillettes of sole (long fillets) in a buttered pan, season with salt and pepper, cover with a glass of white wine, and cook for ten minutes. Then put the sole on a platter, and reduce the wine until nearly dry. Then add a pint of Béarnaise sauce and pour over the fish.

Mock turtle soup. Put in pan six pounds of cut veal bones, two sliced onions and one carrot, and four ounces of butter, and roast until brown. Then add one-quarter pound of flour and brown again. Change to a vessel, add two gallons of water, one can of tomatoes, a bouquet garni, some salt, a spoonful of black pepper berries, and two cloves, and boil for two hours. Add one pint of cooking sherry and boil again for thirty minutes. Skim, and remove the grease from the top, and strain through a cheesecloth. Then take one-quarter of a boiled calf's head and cut in small squares and put in a casserole with one glass of dry sherry wine, a little salt and Cayenne pepper, and boil for five minutes. Now add the strained soup to the calf's head. Before serving add three thin slices of smoked beef tongue cut in small diamond shapes, three chopped hard-boiled eggs, and a truffle cut in small squares.

Roast partridge. Tie a piece of fresh fat pork over the breast of the dressed partridge, season inside and out with salt and pepper, put in roasting pan with a piece of butter, and put in oven. Baste often so the meat will not become dry. It will require about thirty minutes to cook. Serve with lemon and watercress, and bread sauce separate.

Bread sauce, for game. To a pint of boiling milk add one whole onion, a bay leaf with two cloves stuck through it, and one and one-half cups of fresh bread crumbs, and boil for a few minutes. Then remove the onion and bay leaf and cloves, and season with salt and Cayenne pepper. Before serving add two ounces of sweet butter.

Bread crumbs, for game. Put in frying pan four ounces of sweet butter. When just warm add a cupful of fresh bread crumbs, and fry until golden yellow. Drain off the butter (which may be kept for roasting, etc.), and serve the crumbs in a small bowl. This is usually served in addition to bread sauce, with quail, pheasant, partridge, etc.

FEBRUARY 16

BREAKFAST
 Hominy with cream
 Plain scrambled eggs
 Rolls
 English breakfast tea

LUNCHEON
 Crab salad
 Mutton chops, Robinson
 String beans
 Napoleon cake
 Coffee

DINNER
 Pea soup
 Radishes
 Broiled shad, maître d'hôtel
 Roast chicken, au jus
 Hot asparagus, Hollandaise
 Potato croquettes
 Watercress salad
 Peach Mona Lisa
 Assorted cakes
 Coffee

Crab salad. Season the flakes of a crab with salt and pepper, add a spoonful of mayonnaise, and mix. Put a few leaves of lettuce around the inside of a salad bowl, put the crab in the center, cover with mayonnaise, and garnish with a hard-boiled egg cut in four, two fillets of anchovies, and one green olive.

Mutton chops, Robinson. Broil four mutton chops and season well. Cut in four a half dozen chicken livers, season with salt and pepper and fry in butter. Cut up a small can of mushrooms, put in a casserole with the livers, and cover with a cup of sauce Madère. Cook together and pour over the chops.

Watercress salad (1). Clean and wash the watercress well, and season with salt and vinegar.

(2) Use French dressing with a very little oil. Watercress does not require much oil.

Peach Mona Lisa. Make a fancy form in the shape of a peach of vanilla ice cream with a brandied peach in the center. Put a spoonful of raspberry sauce (see raspberry sauce), in the center of a small plate. Put a round piece of sponge cake, about three inches in diameter and one-half inch thick, on the plate. Dust the ice cream peach with some sugar, colored pink, and place on the sponge cake. Stick two sugar peach leaves under the edge of the peach, and serve.

Napoleon cake. When making vol au vent, patty shells, or anything else with puff paste, save the trimmings, roll together and give two turns, in the same manner as when making fresh puff paste. Leave in ice box for one-half hour and then roll out to one-eighth inch in thickness. Put on a pastry pan, prick all over with a fork, and bake in oven until very dry. When done, divide and cut into three strips, and allow to become cold. Put the three strips one on top of the other, with pastry cream between. Glace the top with vanilla icing, and sprinkle a band one-half inch wide along the edge with chopped pistache nuts. Then cut into individual portions about two by four inches in size.

FEBRUARY 17

BREAKFAST
  Grapefruit marmalade
  Boiled eggs
  Buttered toast
  Ceylon tea

LUNCHEON
  Eggs Benedict
  Tripe sauté, Lyonnaise
  Potatoes hashed in cream
  Romaine salad
  Camembert cheese and crackers
  Coffee

DINNER
- Consommé Rachel
- Sardines   Olives
- Boiled sheepshead, cream sauce
- Potatoes Hollandaise
- Roast leg of mutton, currant jelly
- Baked Hubbard squash
- German fried potatoes
- Celery Mayonnaise
- Plum pudding, hard and brandy sauces
- Coffee

Tripe sauté, Lyonnaise. Cut two pounds of tripe in narrow strips. Put in large frying pan four ounces of butter and four sliced onions, and cook until half fried, then add the tripe, which must be dry; season with salt and pepper, and fry until both are of a nice yellow color. Drain off the butter and serve the tripe dry, garnished with quartered lemons and chopped parsley. Vinegar may be served instead of the lemons if desired.

Consommé Rachel (1). Plain consommé garnished with asparagus tips.

(2) Plain consommé garnished with chicken dumplings and small peas.

Boiled sheepshead, cream sauce. Put a whole sheepshead in cold water with one glass of milk, season with salt, and bring to the boiling point. Then put on side of range where it will keep very hot without boiling, and let stand for twenty minutes. Serve on napkin with small boiled potatoes, quartered lemons and parsley. Cream sauce separate.

Plum pudding. One pound of well-chopped beef suet, one pound of sifted flour, one-half pound of bread crumbs; two lemons, both juice and rinds; one pound of brown sugar, four eggs, one-half teaspoonful each of powdered nutmeg, ginger, cloves and cinnamon; one pound of currant raisins; one-half pound each of malaga raisins, orange peel, citron peel and lemon peel, all chopped fine; one cup of molasses, and one-half pint of good brandy. Mix all together in a bowl, putting the liquids in last, making a thick, heavy mixture. Put in a buttered mould or in a cloth, and boil in water, or steam cook, for about three hours. This pudding, if kept in a cool place, will keep indefinitely. Warm the pudding until very hot before serving, sprinkle some powdered sugar over the top, pour on some brandy, and burn.

Brandy sauce. Put in a vessel one-half pint of apricot pulp, made from fresh or preserved fruit; one pint of water, and a half pound of sugar, and boil. Moisten a teaspoonful of arrowroot with a little water and add it to the boiling sauce, stirring so it will not get lumpy. Then strain and add a small glassful of brandy.

Hard sauce. Put in a bowl three-quarters of a pound of sweet butter, one pound of sugar, the white of an egg, and flavor with lemon, vanilla or a little brandy, and work into a cream. Put into a pastry bag with a tube, and dress on a pan in small round shapes. Place in the ice box to get hard.

FEBRUARY 18

BREAKFAST

Waffles

Honey in comb
Boiled eggs
Dry toast
Coffee

LUNCHEON

Grapefruit and oranges en suprême
Chicken broth in cups
Olives
Small sirloin steak, Bordelaise
Potato croquettes
Lettuce and tomato salad
French pastry
Coffee

DINNER

Potage Westmoreland
Oysters à l'ancienne

>
> Chicken pot pie, home style
> Combination salad
> Moka cake
> Demi tasse

Grapefruit and oranges en suprême. Sliced oranges and grapefruit in equal parts, add a little sugar and maraschino, and serve in suprême glasses. Tie a ribbon around the glass, with a nice bow.

Potage Westmoreland. Equal parts of mock turtle soup, thick consommé tapioca, and thick consommé brunoise. Before serving add a glass of dry sherry wine.

Oysters à l'ancienne. Take a dozen oysters on the deep half shell, season with salt and pepper, put a small piece of butter, some chopped parsley, a little lemon juice, and a thin slice of salt pork on each, and bake in a hot oven for about four minutes.

Chicken pot pie, home style. Take a young fat hen and cut up as for fricassee. Wash well and put in a vessel with one quart of water, season with salt, bring to a boil, skim, and add a bouquet garni. After boiling for about thirty minutes remove the bouquet and add twelve small round potatoes, twelve very small onions, and one-quarter pound of parboiled salt pork cut in small squares. Boil all together until well done. Mix in a cup three spoonsful of flour and one-half cup of water, and stir into the stewing chicken. Boil again for about ten minutes, then put in a deep dish, sprinkle with chopped parsley, and when nearly cold cover with thin pie, or puff paste, brush over with the yolk of an egg, and bake in oven until well browned. Serve on a napkin. Dumplings and a few small French carrots may be added before covering with the paste, if desired.

Moka cake. Take three layers of cake and fill between with moka filling. For the filling beat a half pound of sweet butter with a half pound of powdered sugar until it is white and light. Then add the yolks of three eggs, one by one, and a half cup of rich cream, beating until very smooth. Flavor with some strong coffee or coffee extract. Finish the cake by glacing the top with coffee frosting, and decorate with some of the moka filling.

FEBRUARY 19

BREAKFAST
  Stewed prunes
  Scrambled eggs with chives
  Toasted muffins
  Coffee

LUNCHEON
  Canapé of raw meat
  Radishes
  Broiled shad, maître d'hôtel
  Potatoes au gratin
  Cauliflower mayonnaise
  Pont l'Évêque cheese
  Crackers
  Coffee

DINNER
  Cream of Lima beans
  Celery
  Frogs' legs, Jerusalem
  Roast squab chicken
  Individual artichokes, au gratin
  Julienne potatoes
  Endives salad
  Vanilla ice cream
  Assorted cakes
  Coffee

Canapé of raw meat. Take a quarter pound of lean fresh beef tenderloin or sirloin and chop very fine and season with a little salt and pepper. Toast some thin slices of rye or white bread lightly, spread with a little sweet butter, and then spread the chopped meat on top. Serve on a napkin, garnished with quartered lemon and parsley.

Broiled shad, maître d'hôtel. Split a shad, season with salt and pepper, sprinkle with oil, and broil on both sides. Dish up on a platter, cover with maître d'hôtel sauce, and garnish with quartered lemons and parsley.

Cream of Lima beans. Put in a vessel two ounces of butter and one leek cut in small pieces. Simmer for a few minutes, then add one-half cup of flour and simmer again. When hot add one quart of milk and a can of Lima beans, or one pound of fresh beans. When soft strain through a fine sieve, put back in vessel, bring to a boil, and add one-half pint of thick cream and two ounces of best butter. Stir well, and season with salt and pepper and a little Cayenne pepper. In place of the cream, use half chicken broth, light bouillon, veal broth, or half stock and half milk, if desired.

Frogs' legs, Jerusalem. Put in a sauté pan one soupspoonful of chopped celery, three chopped shallots, and three ounces of butter, and simmer for about five minutes. Then add one dozen cut up frogs' legs, season with salt and pepper, and simmer for five minutes. Then add one cup of cream, or one cup of cream sauce, and boil for ten minutes. Serve in chafing dish.

Artichokes au gratin. Remove the leaves from four boiled artichokes and cut the bottoms in slices. Butter four individual shirred egg dishes, put one spoonful of cream sauce in the bottom, then put in the sliced artichokes, season with salt and pepper, cover with cream sauce, sprinkle with grated cheese, put a small piece of butter on top of each, and bake in oven until brown.

FEBRUARY 20

BREAKFAST
  Oatmeal
  Boiled salt mackerel
  Baked potatoes
  Rolls   Coffee

LUNCHEON
  Poached eggs, Rothschild
  Fried chicken, Maryland
  Field salad
  Roquefort cheese, crackers   Coffee

DINNER
  Potage de santé

Salmon, Chambord
Leg of mutton, à la Busse
Spinach with cream   Parisian potatoes
Sliced tomatoes, mayonnaise
Anise seed cake

Poached eggs, Rothschild. Put a spoonful of purée of game on a plate, a poached egg on top, and cover with sauce Périgueux.

Purée of game. After serving roast venison, duck, quail, bear, reindeer, hare, or other game, take the remainder, remove the meat from the bones and mash very fine in a mortar, add just enough thick brown gravy to make a paste, and pass through a fine sieve. Season with salt and pepper, heat well, and use as a garnish.

Salmon, Chambord. Put in a buttered shallow sauce pan two slices of salmon, season with salt and pepper, add half a glass of red wine, and half a glass of stock, bouillon, fish stock or water, cover with buttered paper, and put in the oven and cook until done. With its broth make a sauce Génoise, and add to it one dozen small French mushrooms, one dozen parboiled clams, and one sliced truffle. Pour the sauce over the fish, and garnish with plain-boiled small écrevisses (crayfish).

Leg of mutton, à la Busse. Roast a leg of mutton, serve with its own gravy, and garnish with fresh mushrooms sauté in butter, and onions glacés.

Fresh mushrooms sauté in butter. Clean and wash one pound of fresh mushrooms and dry in a towel. Put in a sauté pan on the range, two ounces of butter; when hot add the mushrooms, season with salt and pepper, and sauté slowly for about ten minutes. Serve on toast with their own gravy, or use as a garnish for entrées, stews, etc.

Onions glacés. Peel one dozen small white onions and put in one quart of cold water with a spoonful of salt. Put on fire, boil for about five minutes, drain off water, and put the onions in a shallow sauté pan with one ounce of butter. Put in oven and roast until brown. Then add one spoonful of meat extract, let them glacé in this for a few minutes, and then serve. If preferred the onions may be glacéd by sprinkling with powdered sugar, and omitting the meat extract. Or take one pint of strong beef consommé and reduce one-half, then add at the same time as the onions, and they will glacé while reducing.

Anise seed cake. One-half pound of sugar, four eggs, one-half pound of flour, and one-half ounce of anise seed. Beat the sugar and eggs together over a slow fire until blood warm, then remove and continue beating until cold and firm. Then add the sifted flour and anise seed. Mix, and lay out on a greased and floured pan in drops about one and one-half inches in diameter. Put in a dry warm place until a crust forms on top (a few hours will be required), and then bake in a slow oven.

Spinach in cream. Boil a peck of well-washed spinach in salted water. Drain off and pound through a fine colander, add two ounces of butter, one cup of thick cream, heat well and serve. Salt and pepper if necessary.

FEBRUARY 21

BREAKFAST
　Baked apples with cream
　Plain omelet
　Rolls
　English breakfast tea

LUNCHEON
　Fillet of herring, mariné
　Potato salad
　Minced tenderloin, à l'estragon
　Mashed potatoes au gratin
　American cheese, crackers　　Coffee

DINNER
　Consommé Florentine　　Ripe olives
　Fillet of sole, Bercy
　Sweetbreads braisé, with peas
　Roast squab, au jus　　Gauffrette potatoes

Cold asparagus, mustard sauce

Coupe Lyonnaise   Assorted cakes   Coffee

Fillet of herring, mariné. Take two marinated herrings, remove the skins and bones, and cut in long strips. Put on platter, strain a little of its own sauce over them, and decorate with sliced lemons.

Minced tenderloin of beef, à l'estragon. Slice one pound of tenderloin of beef in strips one-eighth inch thick and two inches wide, using trimmings or the end piece. Put two ounces of melted butter in frying pan, and when red-hot add the slices of meat, season with salt and pepper, and fry very quickly over a hot fire; about one minute is required. Then remove the meat and sprinkle the pan with one spoonful of flour, and allow to become brown, then add one cup of bouillon or stock, boil for five minutes, add one teaspoonful of chopped fresh tarragon, and test as to seasoning. Then add one ounce of fresh butter and the juice of one lemon. Pour over the fillets, which have been kept warm in a deep dish.

Consommé Florentine. In consommé put some plain boiled spinach cut in small pieces, also thin pancake cut same way. Serve grated cheese separate.

Fillet of sole, Bercy. Put in a buttered flat sauté pan three finely-chopped shallots, the four fillets of a sole on top of the shallots, and a little chopped parsley and chervil on top of the fillets. Season with salt and pepper, add one-half glass of white wine, cover with buttered paper, put on top of the stove and bring to the boiling point. Then put in oven and finish cooking. Remove the fillets to a platter, and put in the sauté pan one pint of white wine sauce, cook for a few minutes, and pour over the fish. Do not strain the sauce. Other fish besides sole may be used if desired.

Roast squab, au jus. Season four squabs, put a piece of fresh fat pork over the breast, and place in roasting pan with one sliced carrot, one onion, one bay leaf, a clove, a few pepper berries, and three ounces of butter. Roast in a hot oven for about thirty-five minutes, basting often. Then put the squabs on a platter, and place the pan on the fire and cook until the butter is clarified. Drain off, add one cup of bouillon and one spoonful of meat extract, reduce one-half, strain, and pour over the squabs. Garnish with watercress.

Waffle potatoes. Cut the potatoes with a special cutter called a potato waffle machine. Put them in warm swimming lard and let it become hot gradually so the potatoes will not become brown too quick. When cooked soft take them out and put them for a second into very hot fat so they will become crisp and golden yellow. Serve on a napkin, sprinkled with salt.

Sybil and Gauffrette potatoes. Same as waffle potatoes.

Coupe Lyonnaise. Fill a glass with vanilla ice cream, and put on top one large marron glacé.

FEBRUARY 22

BREAKFAST
  Orange marmalade
  Buckwheat cakes
  Rolls
  Coffee

LUNCHEON
  Canapé Julia
  Consommé in cups
  Cheese straws
  Sand dabs, meunière
  Broiled chicken on toast
  Sybil potatoes
  Baked Hubbard squash
  Hearts of lettuce
  Meringue glacée à la vanille
  Coffee

DINNER
  Seapuit oysters
  Clear green turtle, au Pemartin
  Crisp celery   Queen olives

> Salted almonds
> Fillet of bass, 1905
> Noisettes of lamb, Ducale
> Breast of chicken with Virginia ham
> Peas au beurre
> Soufflée potatoes
> Alligator pear salad
> Apple Moscovite
> Assorted cakes   Coffee

Canapé Julia. Chop the tail of a lobster very fine and put in a vessel on the range. When hot add one cup of thick cream sauce, bring to a boil, and season with salt and Cayenne pepper. Add the yolks of two eggs, but do not boil, heat just enough to bind the lobster. Make four pieces of toast, put the lobster on top, cover with grated cheese, put a bit of butter on the top of each, and bake in the oven. Serve on napkins, with lemons and parsley.

Noisettes of lamb. Noisettes are cut from the saddle of lamb, free from fat and skin, and in the shape of a small tenderloin steak. Broil or sauté in butter, and serve with Colbert, Béarnaise, or any other meat sauce.

Ducale. Artichoke bottoms filled with French peas, sauce Madère. Use as a garnish for lamb, beef, sweetbreads, etc.

Breast of chicken. Cut the breast from two raw roasting chickens, remove the skin, season with salt and pepper, roll in flour. Put two ounces of butter in a shallow sauté pan, and fry the breasts for about fifteen minutes, or until golden brown. Serve with Virginia ham or bacon, figs, or with sauce Colbert, Madère, cream, etc. If Virginia ham is served take four slices and just heat through on the broiler, or in pan with a little butter. Do not allow to become hard or crisp.

Alligator pear salad. (1). Select ripe, soft pears, but not mushy. Cut in half, remove the stone, fill with French dressing, and serve on cracked ice.

(2). Put in the bottom of a salad bowl some lettuce leaves, scoop out the inside of the pears with a soup spoon, put on the lettuce leaves, and cover with French dressing.

Apple Moscovite. Take four large apples and remove the insides with a sharp spoon, leaving only a firm shell. Put a spoonful of apple sauce on the bottom of the apples. Whip the whites of six eggs very hard, and mix with a half pint of sweet apple sauce. Fill the apples with this, dust over with powdered sugar, and bake in a moderate oven.

FEBRUARY 23

BREAKFAST
  Stewed prunes
  Boiled eggs
  Dry toast
  Coffee

LUNCHEON
  Hors d'oeuvres variés
  Mutton chops, Daumont
  Julienne potatoes
  Swiss cheese and crackers
  Coffee

DINNER
  Potage Kroumir
  Aiguillettes of sole, marinière
  Chicken, Montmorency
  Artichokes with melted butter
  Chiffonnade salad
  Kirschwasser jelly
  Lady fingers
  Coffee

Mutton chops, Daumont. Bread four mutton chops and fry in a flat sauté pan. Dish up on a long platter, and garnish with artichoke bottoms filled with cauliflower. Pour sauce Périgueux around the chops.

Artichokes filled with cauliflower. Remove the leaves and trim the bottoms of four cold artichokes. Cut in four a boiled and well-seasoned cauliflower, squeeze out the water, and use to fill the artichoke bottoms. Cover with a little thick cream sauce, sprinkle with grated cheese, place small bits of butter on top of each, put on a buttered pan with a spoonful of bouillon, and bake in the oven.

Potage Kroumir. One quart of purée of tomato soup mixed with one pint of consommé tapioca.

Aiguillettes of sole, marinière. Take the four fillets from one sole and lay them flat in a buttered pan, sprinkle with three chopped shallots, season with salt and pepper, add one-half glass of white wine, one-half cup of stock or water, cover with buttered paper, and bring to a boil on top of the stove. Then put in oven and cook for about seven minutes. Put the fillets on a platter, and reduce the broth until nearly dry. Then add two cups of white wine sauce and boil for a minute. Bind the sauce with the yolk of an egg mixed with a spoonful of cream, add a little chopped chives, and pour over the fish.

Chicken sauté, Montmorency. Joint a chicken, season with salt and pepper, put three ounces of butter in a sauté pan and sauté the chicken. When done remove the chicken to a platter, and put in the pan one cup of brown gravy or sauce Madère, and one can of French mushrooms. Boil for a few minutes. Then pour over the chicken. Garnish with croustades filled with small French peas.

Croustades. One cup of flour, one cup of milk, the whites of three eggs, a teaspoonful of olive oil, a teaspoonful of corn starch, and a little salt. Mix well and strain. Keep the croustade iron very hot in swimming lard. Dip the iron in the dough for a few seconds, then dip in the swimming lard, coated with the dough, and fry until a nice golden color. Take out, and when cold the croustades will be very crisp. Croustade irons can be obtained in any first-class store.

FEBRUARY 24

BREAKFAST
  Grapefruit with cherries
  Omelet with ham
  Rolls
  Coffee

LUNCHEON
  Eggs Talleyrand
  Oysters à la Hyde
  French pastry
  Coffee

DINNER
  Cream of frogs' legs
  Olives
  Scallops, Newburg
  Roast Easter kid, mint sauce
  Sweetbreads sauté, with green peas
  Endives salad
  Fancy ice cream
  Assorted cakes
  Coffee

Eggs Talleyrand. Trim the bottoms of four fresh artichokes and put a little terrine de foie gras in each, and keep hot. Put a poached egg on top of each and cover with sauce Périgueux.

Cream of frogs' legs. Take the backs and front legs of two dozen frogs, reserving the hind legs for an entrée. Put in vessel with two quarts of bouillon or chicken broth, and boil for thirty minutes. Then take one-half pound of rice flour and mix with one pint of cream. Let it run into the boiling soup, and cook for ten minutes. Strain through a fine colander, put back in the vessel, season with salt and a little Cayenne pepper, and add three ounces of sweet butter. Stir the soup so the butter will melt slowly. Serve croûtons soufflés separate.

Scallops, Newburg. Put one pint of scallops in a sauté pan with one ounce of butter, season with salt and pepper, and sauté for about three minutes over a hot fire; then drain off and add one pint of sauce Newburg. Do not cook further, and serve in chafing dish.

Roast Easter kid. Kid when young is a delicious morsel. Prepare in the same manner as lamb for roasting.

Sweet potatoes sauté. Peel and slice two large boiled sweet potatoes. Put three ounces of butter in a sauté pan, when hot add the potatoes and sauté until nice and brown. Season with salt and pepper.

FEBRUARY 25

BREAKFAST
Waffles
Honey
Coffee

LUNCHEON
Poached eggs, Martha
Hungarian beef goulash
Noodles, Polonaise
Savarin Chantilly
Coffee

DINNER
Consommé Colbert
Broiled Alaska candlefish
Sweetbreads, Théodora
Roast ribs of beef, au jus
Saratoga potatoes
Celery Victor
Fruit cake

Coffee

Poached eggs, Martha. On top of four pieces of toast put some lobster croquette preparation in a layer about one-quarter of an inch thick, put a piece of butter on top of each, and bake in oven. Put a poached egg on top and cover with cream sauce.

Noodles, Polonaise. On a large platter put one pound of plain boiled noodles. In a frying pan put one-quarter pound of butter, and one-half cup of fresh bread crumbs. Fry until golden brown, and pour over the noodles.

Consommé Colbert. Equal parts of carrots, turnips, peas, string beans, cauliflower, and flageolet beans. Cut the carrots and turnips in small squares. Boil the cauliflower and cut off the small flowers. Then put all in hot consommé, with one poached egg to each person. Add a little chopped chervil before serving.

Broiled Alaska candlefish. As this fish is very oily it is better broiled. Season with salt and pepper, and serve on platter, with plenty of lemon and parsley in branches.

Sweetbreads, Théodora. Split four large sweetbreads, fill with chicken forcemeat, and braise them. Serve with sauce Madère, and garnish with stuffed fresh mushrooms.

Fruit cake (white). One pound each of butter, sugar and flour, one-half teaspoonful of baking powder, ten eggs, one-quarter pound of currant sultana raisins, one pony of rum, and one-quarter pound of chopped glacé fruits. Work the butter and the sugar together until creamy, then add the eggs two by two, and work well, then add the rum, and finally the flour, baking powder and fruit. Mix lightly, and bake in a buttered pan lined with paper.

FEBRUARY 26

BREAKFAST	LUNCHEON
Stewed prunes	Eggs à la Colonel
Boiled eggs	English lamb chops, Tavern
Buttered toast	Lettuce salad
Coffee	Pont l'évêque cheese
	Crackers
	Coffee

DINNER
Cream of rice
Ripe olives
Rock cod, en court bouillon
Potatoes nature
Squab chicken sauté, Sutro
Olivette potatoes
Endives salad
Orange soufflé, St. Francis
Assorted cakes
Coffee

Eggs à la Colonel. Cut two tomatoes in half, squeeze out the juice, bread them, and fry. Put a poached egg on top of each piece, and cover with sauce Madère with fresh mushrooms.

English lamb chops, Tavern. Broil an English lamb chop until nearly done, then put in an earthern casserole, with some sauté potatoes on one side and some stewed lamb kidneys on the other. Put in the oven for a minute or two, and serve with chopped parsley on top.

English mutton chop, Tavern. Same as English lamb chop, Tavern.

Rock cod, en court bouillon. Put in a flat pan three spoonsful of olive oil, one onion sliced very fine, three sliced green and one red pepper, one bouquet garni, and about five pounds of codfish cut in slices two inches thick. Season with salt and pepper, add two glasses of white wine and one pint of water, and a little chopped parsley. Simmer slowly for about forty minutes. Remove the bouquet garni, and serve on a deep platter with broth and all. Any fish may be prepared in the same manner.

Squab chicken sauté, Sutro. Cut two squab chickens in six pieces each. Two legs, two wings, and the breast and carcass split. Season with salt and pepper, and sauté in pan with two ounces of butter. Prepare as follows: Two fresh artichoke bottoms boiled and cut in four; one-half pound of fresh mushrooms sauté in butter; one can of cèpes sauté in butter; the livers of the chickens whole, and one parboiled sweetbread sliced and sauté in butter. Mix all together with the chicken, season well, and add some chopped parsley and chives.

Orange Soufflé, St. Francis. Cut "lids" from the tops of four large oranges and remove the insides. Have the openings about an inch and one-half in diameter. Fill about one-third full with some sliced fresh fruit, such as oranges, apples, bananas, pineapple, etc. Then add a few drops of maraschino, fill another third with vanilla ice cream. Beat the whites of six eggs until stiff, mixed with one-half pound of sugar and the grated rind of an orange, and fill the final third of the orange. Dust with powdered sugar, and brown on top in a very hot oven. It will take but a second to brown, and they should be served at once.

FEBRUARY 27

BREAKFAST	LUNCHEON
Orange marmalade	Omelet with Virginia ham and peppers
Ham and eggs	Calf's head, vinaigrette
Corn muffins	Baked potatoes
Coffee	Apricot layer cake
	Coffee

DINNER

Strained gumbo soup, in cups
Radishes
Barracouda, maître d'hôtel
Stuffed capon, Bruxelloise
Asparagus, Hollandaise
Champs Élysées potatoes
Hearts of romaine, Roquefort dressing
Chocolate parfait
Lady fingers
Coffee

Omelet with Virginia ham and peppers. Cut two slices of Virginia ham and one green pepper in small squares, put in frying pan with one ounce of butter, and simmer for about two minutes. Add eight beaten eggs and two red peppers cut in small squares, season with salt and pepper, and proceed in the same manner as for a plain omelet.

Calf's head, vinaigrette. Dish up on a napkin some boiled calf's head with the brains and the tongue sliced. Garnish the platter with pickles, pickled beets, quartered lemons, parsley in branches, and two hard-boiled eggs cut in two. Serve vinaigrette sauce separate.

Strained gumbo soup, in cups. Make a chicken okra soup, strain through cheese cloth, and serve in cups.

Stuffed capon, Bruxelloise. Soak half of a loaf of white bread in milk, then squeeze out the milk, mince fine, add salt and pepper, a little chopped parsley, one pound of finely chopped salted almonds, and one egg. Mix well together and fill the capon. Tie a slice of fresh fat pork over the breast, and roast in the same manner as chicken or other fowl.

Layer cake. Eight eggs, one-half pound of flour, one-quarter pound of melted butter, and a few drops of vanilla extract. Beat the eggs with the sugar over a slow fire until thoroughly warm, then take off the range and continue beating until cold. Put in the flour, mixing lightly, and add the melted butter and vanilla extract. Bake in buttered flat tin cake moulds, for about ten minutes.

French layer cake. The same as above with the exception that it is baked in one thick cake and then cut into layers.

Chocolate layer cake. Use three or four layers, filling between with chocolate cream. Glacé with chocolate frosting, and decorate the top with glacé fruits. See pastry cream for directions for filling.

Apricot layer cake. Same as chocolate layer cake, but fill with apricot marmalade, glacé the top with vanilla frosting, and decorate with glacé fruit.

FEBRUARY 28

BREAKFAST
- Shredded wheat with cream
- Crescents
- Cocoa

LUNCHEON
- Eggs à la Reine
- Tripe à la mode de Caën
- Camembert cheese and crackers
- Coffee

DINNER
- Consommé d'Orleans
- Celery
- Fillet of sole, Victoria
- Leg of mutton, Réforme
- Carrots, Vichy
- Potato salad
- Peach Melba
- Assorted cakes
- Coffee

Poached eggs, à la Reine. Spread some purée de foie gras on a piece of toast. Put a poached egg on top, cover with cream sauce, and sprinkle with finely chopped truffles. After the truffles have been chopped put in a napkin and squeeze out the juice, and then chop again. They will then be dry, and easy to sprinkle.

Fillet of sole, Victoria. Put four fillets in a buttered sauté pan, season with salt and pepper, add one-half glass of white wine. When done put on platter and pour a lobster sauce over the fish, with lobster and truffles cut in small squares, in it.

Leg of mutton, Réforme. Roast a leg of mutton, and serve the following sauce separate: Ham, tongue, pickles, mushrooms, and chicken in equal parts, cut Julienne style, and mixed with sauce poivrade.

Sauce poivrade. Crush one-half cup of black pepper berries and put in vessel with one dozen chopped shallots, a little parsley, and one pint of white wine vinegar. Boil and reduce until nearly dry, then add one quart of brown sauce, or sauce Madère, and boil for five minutes, then strain, and stir in three ounces of sweet butter slowly.

Tripe à la mode de Caën. Parboil eight pounds of raw tripe and four ox feet. Cut both the tripe and the feet in pieces two inches square. Chop one pound of raw beef suet and four large onions very fine. Put in an earthen pot half of the suet and onions, then half of the tripe and feet, then the remainder of the suet and onions, followed by the rest of the tripe and feet. Season with salt and pepper, add one bouquet garni, one-half pint of brandy, one pint of white wine, and fill the remainder of the space in the pot with water. Put a cover on the pot and seal with any kind of paste or dough, so that no air or steam can escape. Then put the pot in a moderate oven and leave for about eight hours; then take out of oven, take off the cover, and remove the bouquet garni. If there should be too much fat on top a little may be taken off. Ordinarily there will not be too much. Season to taste with salt and pepper, add one-half pint of dry apple cider and one glass of brandy, and boil for two minutes. Serve hot. The proper way to serve tripe à la mode de Caën is in small individual earthen pots, on a large plate, with red-hot ashes under the pot.

MARCH 1

BREAKFAST
  Strawberries with cream
  Boiled eggs
  Dry toast
  Coffee

LUNCHEON
  Grapefruit en suprême
  Consommé in cups
  Cheese straws
  Sweet-and-sour beef tongue
  String beans
  Mashed potatoes
  Chocolate éclairs   Coffee

DINNER
  Oysters on half shell
  Onion soup au gratin
  Kingfish sauté, meunière
  Roast chicken
  Succotash
  Potato cakes
  Escarole salad
  Corn meal pudding   Coffee

Sweet-and-sour sauce. Procure one-half pound of unsweetened spiced fish cake from your grocer, break it in small pieces, put in a bowl, cover with one pint of vinegar and one pound of brown sugar. Soak for about an hour, then stir well, and add one cup of fish broth or meat stock, depending upon whether it is to be used for fish or meat. Season with salt and a little Cayenne pepper, then add one pound of seedless raisins, and boil again for five minutes.

Sweet-and-sour beef tongue. Boil a fresh beef tongue in the same manner as boiled beef. When done cut in thin slices, put in a flat pan, cover with sweet-and-sour sauce, and simmer for five minutes. Serve on a platter covered with the sauce.

Omelette Suzanne. Cut six macaroons in four and mix with a little whipped cream. Cut six lady fingers in two and sprinkle with powdered cocoa and powdered sugar. Melt some Bar le Duc jelly. Make an omelet in the usual manner, powder with plenty of sugar, and burn bands across the top with a hot iron. At one end of the omelet place the lady fingers, at the other end the macaroons, and pour some of the Bar le Duc jelly on each side. Pour a pony of Chartreuse over the omelet, then a pony of fine champagne, and light it.

Cheese straws. Roll out some puff paste (a good way to utilize any trimmings you may have) very thin, about one-eighth inch. Wash the top with eggs and spread with grated Parmesan cheese mixed with a little Cayenne pepper. Cut in narrow strips, one-half inch by six, lay on a baking pan and bake in a moderate oven until brown and crisp.

Onion soup, au gratin. Slice three onions very fine, put in a casserole with three ounces of butter, put on the cover, and simmer until of a golden color. Then add one quart of consommé, stock or any good broth (consommé preferred), season well, and boil for five minutes. Slice three rolls very thin and put in oven and allow to remain until brown and dry, like toast. Put the soup in an earthen casserole, float the slices of rolls on top, spread a cup of grated cheese over the bread, put in a hot oven and cook until brown on top. Serve very hot.

Potato cakes. Whenever there is mashed potatoes left over, make into little cakes about one inch thick and two inches in diameter, roll in flour, and fry in pan with a little butter, until brown on both sides. If the potato should be too thin add the raw yolk of an egg.

MARCH 2

BREAKFAST
 Oatmeal with cream
 Broiled finnan haddie

LUNCHEON
 Eggs Bordelaise
 Lamb chops, Victor Hugo

Lyonnaise potatoes Julienne potatoes
Rolls Stewed tomatoes
Coffee Brie cheese, crackers Coffee

DINNER

Cream of lettuce Radishes
Scallops, Mornay
Croustades financière
Roast leg of mutton, currant jelly
Potato croquettes
Cold asparagus, mustard sauce
Fruit salad, au marasquin
Lady fingers Coffee

Eggs Bordelaise. Fry the eggs in oil, put on toast, cover with Bordelaise sauce, and lay two slices of truffle on each egg.

Lamb chops, Victor Hugo. Broil or sauté six lamb chops on one side only, and allow to become cold. Grate two horseradish roots and put in a sauce pot with two ounces of butter, and simmer. Then add one cup of thick cream sauce, and bring to a boil; season well and bind with the yolks of two eggs. When this stuffing is cold put on top of the chops, make smooth with a knife, sprinkle with a little grated Parmesan cheese mixed with bread crumbs, put small bits of butter on each chop, place on a buttered pan, and put in a hot oven, so they will cook from the bottom. Cook until the tops are nice and brown, and serve on a platter with brown gravy, and two slices of truffle on each.

Cream of lettuce. Take the trimmings of six heads of lettuce, in volume about the same as two heads of lettuce, wash well and cut in small bits. Take two quarts of chicken broth, or any kind of clear broth or stock, add the lettuce to it and boil for thirty minutes. Put in a separate vessel four ounces of butter, and heat; add three spoonfuls of flour and heat again; add the broth containing the lettuce and boil for ten minutes. Boil a pint of cream, mix with the soup, and strain through a fine sieve. Put back in vessel, add two or three ounces of sweet butter, and stir until the butter is melted. Season with salt and a little Cayenne pepper.

Scallops, Mornay. Put one pint of scallops in a sauté pan with an ounce of butter, season with salt and pepper, and heat through. Then remove the juice and add one cup of thick cream sauce, mix well, put in a deep dish, sprinkle with grated Parmesan or Swiss cheese, put small bits of butter on top, and bake in hot oven until brown.

Croustades financière. Make a financière, but cut a little smaller than for garniture. Fill the croustades, and serve on napkin with parsley in branches.

Financière (garniture). Cut two parboiled sweetbreads in slices, and sauté in butter; add one-half can of French mushrooms, or one-quarter pound of fresh mushrooms cut in two and sautéed, rooster combs and kidneys, sliced truffles, small chicken dumplings, and a few green olives with the stones removed. Put all in a casserole, season well, add a pint of good Madeira sauce, and serve hot. This garnish may be used for filling croustades, vol au vents, small patties, or as an entrée.

MARCH 3

BREAKFAST
  Griddle cakes with
    maple syrup
  Buttered toast
  Oolong tea

LUNCHEON
  Poached eggs, Monnet Sully
  Imported Frankfort sausages
  Sauerkraut
  Boiled potatoes
  Limberger cheese and crackers
  Coffee

DINNER
  Toke Point oysters
  Pannade soup
  Boiled sea bass,

SUPPER
  Golden buck

Hollandaise
Potatoes nature
Chicken sauté, Salonika
Peas au cerfeuil
Chiffonnade salad
Biscuit glacé
Assorted cakes
Coffee

Poached eggs, Monnet Sully. Place a poached egg on a canapé of chicken and pour Béarnaise sauce over it.

Canapé of chicken. Take the breast of a boiled fowl and chop very fine, season with salt and pepper, mix well with two ounces of sweet butter, and spread on fresh toast.

Pannade soup. Take a half loaf of stale white bread, or some rolls, and put in a pot with three pints of water, season with salt and pepper, add one-quarter of a pound of butter, cover, and boil slowly for one hour. It will then be of the consistency of gruel. Mix the yolks of two eggs with a cup of cream and a half cup of milk, and stir slowly into the boiling soup. This is an excellent plain soup, and fine for the digestion.

Peas au cerfeuil. Put three ounces of butter in a casserole, add one quart of parboiled peas, some chopped chervil (cerfeuil), season with salt and a pinch of sugar, and simmer for five minutes.

Boiled sea bass, Hollandaise. Put a whole sea bass, including the head and tail, in a fish kettle, in cold water. Season with salt, some whole black pepper berries, and a bouquet garni. Add one sliced onion, and one carrot, bring to a boil and then set on the side for fifteen minutes. Serve on a napkin with small boiled potatoes, quartered lemons and parsley. Hollandaise sauce separate.

Fried artichokes. Trim the bottoms of six boiled artichokes, cut in four, put in flour, then in milk, then in beaten egg, then in fresh bread crumbs, and fry in swimming fat. Serve on napkin with lemon and parsley.

Chicken sauté, Salonika. Joint a chicken and season with salt and pepper. Put two spoonfuls of olive oil in a sauté pan, and when very hot add the chicken. Sauté until nice and brown, then add one chopped shallot. When the shallot is hot pour off the oil, add one cup of brown gravy, and simmer for five minutes. Dish up on a flat platter, pour the sauce over it, sprinkle with chopped parsley, and garnish both ends of the platter with fried artichokes.

Golden buck. A Welsh rabbit with a poached egg on top.

MARCH 4

BREAKFAST
  Sliced pineapple
  Bacon and eggs
  Rolls
  Coffee

LUNCHEON
  Mussels marinière
  Reindeer chop, port wine sauce
  Sweet potatoes, sauté
  Lettuce braisé
  Waldorf salad
  French pastry
  Coffee

DINNER
  California oyster cocktail
  Ox tail soup, English style
  Frogs' legs, Jerusalem
  Filet mignon, Bayard
  Flageolet beans
  Sybil potatoes
  Hearts of lettuce

SUPPER
  Hangtown fry

Raspberry water ice
Assorted cakes
Coffee

Sauce marinière. Cut fine six shallots, put in casserole with one ounce of butter, and simmer just enough to have the shallots hot, then add one glass of white wine and boil until reduced nearly dry. Then add one pint of sauce Allemande and boil for five minutes. Season with salt and pepper, and sprinkle with a little chopped parsley and chives.

Sauce Allemande. Put four ounces of butter and three spoonfuls of flour in a casserole and place on the stove. When hot add one quart of chicken or veal broth, and boil for twenty minutes, then bind with the yolks of three eggs mixed with one-half cup of thick cream. Strain and season well with salt and a little Cayenne pepper.

Mussels, marinière. Wash the mussels well to free them from all sand. Put in casserole with one-half glass of white wine and one cup of water, bring to the boiling point, then add six chopped shallots, and boil until the mussels are open. Remove the mussels to another vessel, strain the broth, and reduce. Then add one pint of sauce marinière, and pour over the mussels. The mussels may be served with the entire shells attached; on the half shell, or removed from the shells altogether, after they have been boiled.

Reindeer chop. Reindeer should be hung up for at least two weeks before being cooked, otherwise it will be very tough. The meat is very good, and easily prepared. Salt and pepper the chops, roll in olive oil, and broil; or fry in frying pan, in the same manner as any other kind of chop or steak. Serve with maître d'hôtel, or some fancy meat sauce.

Port wine sauce. Take the brown gravy from a roast, or use any kind of brown sauce, or sauce Madère; add one glass of port wine and boil for two minutes. This sauce is excellent with game. If a sweeter sauce is desired one-half cup of hot currant jelly may be added.

Filet mignon, Bayard. Sauté in butter, or broil, small tenderloin steaks, place on toast, spread with purée de foie gras, cover with sauce Madère with sliced truffles, and garnish with small round chicken croquettes.

Hangtown fry. Mix plain scrambled eggs with one dozen small fried California oysters.

MARCH 5

BREAKFAST
  Pearl grits with cream
  Broiled smoked salmon
  Toast Melba
  Coffee

LUNCHEON
  Eggs, Meyerbeer
  Paprika schnitzel with spätzel
  Gorgonzola cheese with crackers
  Coffee

DINNER
  Cream of bananas
  Ripe California olives
  Fillet of bass, Nanon
  Chicken sauté, Créole
  Boiled rice
  Escarole and chicory salad
  Nesselrode pudding
  Assorted cakes
  Coffee

Pearl grits. To one quart of boiling water add eight ounces of pearl grits, season with salt, and boil for twenty minutes. Serve cream separate.

Eggs, Meyerbeer. For each person cook two eggs on a shirred egg dish. Have the eggs very soft. Place a broiled split lamb's kidney in the center of each dish and cover with a little sauce Madère. Place two slices of truffle on top. Season well.

Broiled smoked salmon. Slice the salmon about one-half inch thick, roll in olive oil, and broil. When done put on platter, cover with maître d'hôtel sauce, and garnish with quartered lemons and parsley.

Toast Melba. Cut some white bread in very thin slices, trim, put on a pan and bake in the oven until brown.

Paprika schnitzel. Cut four slices from a leg of veal. The slices should be about one-half inch thick, two and one-half inches wide and six inches long. Season them with salt and paprika. Melt three ounces of butter in a sauté pan, when hot put the slices of meat in the pan and sauté for about five minutes. Then add one cup of very thick cream, a little more salt, one teaspoonful of paprika, and simmer for five minutes. If the sauce should be too thin add one spoonful of cream sauce and simmer for a few minutes.

Nesselrode pudding. Beat over the fire the yolks of eight eggs, one-half pound of sugar, and one pony of good rum, until light and creamy. Then remove from the fire and continue beating until cold. Then add one quart of whipped cream and one-half pound of broken marrons glacés. Mix well, and put in one large, or in individual moulds, pack in ice and salt, and leave until hard. It will require about two hours to freeze. To serve, remove from mould, decorate the top with a marron glacé, and pour maraschino sauce around the bottom of the pudding.

Spätzel. These are small flour dumplings, but made harder than the usual dumpling. Mix well one cup of flour, one whole egg and the yolk of an egg, one-third of a cup of milk, a little salt and pepper, and a very little grated nutmeg. Form in small bits and drop into boiling salted water and boil for about five minutes, then pour off the water. In a frying pan put two ounces of butter and cook until brown, then pour over the spätzel and mix.

Cream of bananas. Make a cream of chicken soup, heat six bananas in it, and strain through a fine sieve.

MARCH 6

BREAKFAST
Bar le Duc jelly
Spanish omelet
Dry toast
Chocolate with whipped cream

LUNCHEON
Grapefruit with cherries
Fried tomcods, Tartar sauce
Turkeys' livers en brochette
Flageolet beans
French pastry
Coffee

DINNER
Consommé royal
Soft clams, bâtelière
Roast turkey, cranberry sauce
Sweet potato croquettes
Asparagus Hollandaise
Chiffonnade salad
Mince pie
American cheese
Coffee

Spanish omelet. Make a plain omelet and pour one cup of Créole sauce around it.

Fried tomcods. Clean eight tomcods, wash well, and dry with a towel. Roll in milk, then in flour, and fry in swimming fat for about five minutes, or until nice and brown. The fat must be very hot. Serve on a napkin with fried parsley, quartered lemons, and Tartar sauce separate.

Turkeys' livers en brochette. Take three turkey livers and cut each in four slices. Broil three slices of bacon, and cut in four pieces also. Now stick a piece of liver on a skewer, then a piece of bacon, then another piece of liver, then another piece of bacon, and so continue until the skewer is full. Season with salt and pepper, roll in fresh bread crumbs, sprinkle with olive oil, and broil. When done on all sides place on a piece of toast, put some maître d'hôtel sauce over it, and garnish with quarters of lemon and water-cress.

Clams bâtelière. Separate the bellies from one dozen soft clams and put them back in their half shells. Season with salt and pepper, cover with maître d'hôtel sauce, put a thin slice of salt pork over the top, and place in oven and bake. Garnish with quartered lemon and parsley.

Roast turkey. Season the turkey well, fill with any kind of stuffing, and roast in the same manner as roast turkey stuffed with chestnuts.

MARCH 7

BREAKFAST
- Fresh strawberries with cream
- Boiled eggs
- Rolls
- Coffee

LUNCHEON
- Eggs Sarah Bernhardt
- Reindeer stew
- Mashed potatoes
- Camembert cheese and crackers
- Coffee

DINNER
- Cherrystone oysters on half shell
- Cream of farina
- Fillet of turbot, Bonnefoy
- Lamb chops, charcutière
- Succotash
- French fried potatoes
- Romaine salad
- Fancy ice cream
- Assorted cakes   Coffee

Eggs Sarah Bernhardt. Cut six hard-boiled eggs in two, remove the yolks, mash them up and mix with a little salt, pepper, celery salt, one spoonful of fresh bread crumbs, one spoonful of chopped chicken meat, and the yolk of one raw egg. Stuff the halved whites of eggs with this, put on a buttered dish and place in the oven for four minutes. Dress on a silver platter, and cover with sauce Périgueux.

Sauce Périgueux. Chop a small can of truffles and put in a casserole with one glass of Madeira, and reduce until nearly dry. Then add one pint of brown gravy and season with salt and Cayenne pepper.

Sauce Périgord. Slice one small can of truffles, put in casserole with one glass of Madeira or sherry wine, reduce, add one pint of brown gravy and boil again for twelve minutes. Season with salt and Cayenne pepper.

Reindeer stew. Cut about five pounds of shoulder and breast of reindeer in pieces two inches square. Put in sauté pan with one-quarter pound of butter, season with salt and pepper, and sauté until nice and brown. Then add two spoonfuls of flour and simmer until the flour is slightly brown; add one pint of claret and one quart of boiling water, a bouquet garni, and bring to a boil; skim, cover and let slowly cook until nearly done. Sauté in butter twelve heads of fresh mushrooms, and parboil twelve very small potatoes and fry in butter, add them to the stew and cook until soft. Season well with salt and pepper.

Cream of farina. Boil one pound of farina in one quart of milk. When done add one pint of well-seasoned chicken broth, and strain through a fine sieve. Put back in pot, add two ounces of sweet butter and one pint of boiling cream. Season with salt and a little Cayenne pepper.

Fillet of turbot, Bonnefoy. Cut the turbot in fillets about one and one-half inches wide and three inches long. Put in sauté pan, season with salt and pepper, add six very finely chopped shallots, one small can of mushrooms, or a half pound of fresh mushrooms, and one glass of claret. Cover with buttered manilla paper, put in oven and simmer for ten minutes, then remove the fish to a platter. Put the pan with the gravy on the fire, add one pint of tomato sauce and boil for five minutes. Then stir in well one ounce of good butter, and pour over the fish.

Lamb chops, charcutière. Broil some lamb chops and cover with brown sauce with which has been mixed some sliced pickle and sliced green olives in equal parts. Season the sauce well.

MARCH 8

BREAKFAST
  Stewed prunes
  Scrambled eggs with bacon
  Buttered toast
  English breakfast tea

LUNCHEON
  Canapé of fresh caviar
  Consommé in cups
  Cheese straws
  Spring lamb Irish stew
  Cream puffs
  Coffee

DINNER
  Purée d'Artois (soup)
  Salted pecans
  Broiled shad, Albert
  Chicken à l'Estragon
  Potatoes au gratin
  Artichokes, sauce Hollandaise
  Omelette soufflée
  Coffee

Purée d'Artois. Same as purée of peas.

Broiled shad, Albert. Broiled shad with horseradish sauce.

Chicken à l'Estragon. Boil a whole chicken in a quart of water with salt and a bouquet garni. When done pull the skin off but leave the chicken whole. Make the sauce in the following manner: Put three ounces of butter in a casserole, when hot add two and one-half spoonfuls of flour and one and one-half pints of the chicken broth, boil for ten minutes, add a little chopped tarragon and boil for another ten minutes. Bind with the yolks of two eggs and a half cup of cream, strain, and season with salt and Cayenne pepper. Pour the sauce over the chicken, and lay a few leaves of tarragon on top.

Omelette soufflée. Mix a cup of powdered sugar with the yolks of two eggs and the inside of a vanilla bean, and beat until it is light and fluffy. Beat the whites of eight eggs until they are very stiff, then add to the batter, mixing lightly. Place this on a buttered silver platter that has been dusted with powdered sugar, form into a fancy shape, decorate through a pastry bag with some of the same preparation, dust with powdered sugar, and bake in a rather hot oven for about ten minutes.

Omelette soufflée en surprise. Cut a piece of sponge cake into an oval shape about one-half inch thick, three inches wide and six inches long. Put on top of the cake one pint of vanilla ice cream that has been frozen very hard, cover with omelette soufflée preparation, decorate in the same manner as above, dust with powdered sugar, and bake in a very hot oven for two minutes.

MARCH 9

BREAKFAST
  Orange marmalade
  Boiled eggs
  Dry toast
  Ceylon tea

LUNCHEON
  Eggs Maltaise
  Calf's head, à la Française
  Plain boiled potatoes
  Brie cheese and crackers   Coffee

DINNER

>Cream of green corn
>Matelote of fish
>Leg of mutton, Bretonne
>Field salad
>Sand tart   Coffee

Eggs Maltaise. Fill a croustade with purée of fresh mushrooms, put a poached egg on top, and cover with cream sauce.

Calf's head, à la Française. Boil a calf's head, with the tongue and brains, and dish up on a china platter. Make a macédoine of vegetables as follows: Boil in salt water a carrot and a turnip, and when cold cut up in small dices. Add one-half pound of cold cooked string beans cut in pieces about one-half inch long, one-quarter pound of boiled peas, and one-half can of flageolet beans. Put this macédoine in a salad bowl, add one teaspoonful of salt, one-half teaspoonful of fresh-ground black pepper, a little parsley and chervil, one-half cup of white wine vinegar, and one and one-half cups of olive oil. Mix well and pour over the calf's head.

Cream of green corn. Soak five pounds of green corn in cold water over night. Then put on fire in pot with one-half gallon of bouillon, and cook until soft. Then strain through a fine sieve, put back in pot, add one quart of boiling cream, and season with salt and a little Cayenne pepper. Before serving add four ounces of sweet butter, and stir well until melted.

White beans, Bretonne. Soak 3 pounds of white beans in cold water over night. Put in a vessel with three quarts of water, a ham bone, a bouquet garni, and a small handful of salt. Boil until soft, then remove the ham bone and bouquet, and drain off the water. Chop three large onions very fine, put in casserole with three ounces of butter, and simmer until cooked, then add a teaspoonful of chopped garlic and heat through, pour in a cupful of purée of tomatoes and some chopped parsley, add the beans, season well with fresh-ground black pepper, and cook for ten minutes.

Leg of mutton, Bretonne. Roast leg of mutton garnished with beans Bretonne.

Matelote of fish. Take the solid meat of any kind of fresh fish such as bass, carp, perch, etc., and cut about four pounds in slices two inches thick. Put in buttered pan, season with salt and pepper, add one pint of claret, one cup of stock, fish broth, or water, and a bouquet garni. Cover, put over a slow fire and boil for about twenty minutes, or until soft. Put the fish in a deep dish, cover with matelote sauce, and garnish with boiled écrevisses. To make the matelote sauce put three ounces of butter in a casserole and allow to become hot. Then add two spoonfuls of flour, heat well, and then pour in the strained broth from the fish, boil for ten minutes, add one spoonful of meat extract and one teaspoonful of essence of anchovies, and strain. Peel one dozen very small white onions, parboil then and fry in butter until soft. Add the onions and one can of French mushrooms to the sauce, season well, and boil.

Sand tart (Sablé). One pound of sugar, one pound of flour, the yolks of five eggs, six ounces of butter, and three tablespoonfuls of thick sour milk in which has been dissolved one pinch of soda. Mix to a hard dough and roll very thin. Beat the whites of two eggs and use to moisten the top of the rolled dough. Cut in the desired shape, sprinkle with sugar mixed with a little powdered cinnamon and chopped almonds, put on buttered pan and bake quick.

MARCH 10

BREAKFAST
- Sliced bananas with cream
- Broiled finnan haddie
- Baked potatoes
- Rolls
- Coffee

LUNCHEON
- Eggs Renaissance
- Mutton chops, Signora
- Fried egg plant
- Romaine salad
- Meringued peaches   Coffee

DINNER

    Mock turtle soup
    Oysters, Victor
    Croustades Laguipierre
    Roast capon, au jus
    Fresh asparagus, Hollandaise
    Champs Elysées potatoes
    Escarole salad
    Fancy ice cream
    Assorted cakes   Coffee

Eggs Renaissance. Put a little cream sauce in the bottom of a buttered cocotte dish, add a raw egg, season with salt and pepper, then add a few sliced canned mushrooms and sliced truffles, cover with cream sauce, sprinkle with grated cheese, put bits of butter on top, and bake in oven.

Mutton chops, Signora. Split open four mutton chops, season with salt and pepper, put three slices of truffle in each chop and fold together, roll in flour, then in beaten egg, and finally in bread crumbs. Fry the chops for ten minutes in hot melted butter. Serve cream sauce to which has been added some chopped truffles.

Meringued peaches. (Pêche meringuée.) Cook one quarter pound of rice in one quart of milk for about one-half hour. The rice should be stiff when done. Add one pony of cream, one ounce of butter, two ounces of sugar, and mix well. Spread on a dish about one inch deep, and place on top some halved preserved peaches, or some fresh peaches cooked in syrup. Make a meringue paste with the whites of four eggs beaten stiff and a half pound of sugar. Cover the peaches with the meringue, using a pastry bag with a fancy tube. Dust over with powdered sugar, and bake in a rather cool oven until it becomes a little dry and brown.

Oysters Victor. Wash the heads of three fresh mushrooms, dry them in a towel, and chop very fine, also chop very fine six walnuts and put in salad bowl with the mushrooms, season with salt and pepper, add three ounces of butter and a little chopped parsley, and mix well together. Spread this paste on top of a dozen oysters on the half shell, and bake in oven for about five minutes. Serve with halves of lemon.

Croustades Laguipierre. Use equal parts of chickens' livers, sauté in butter, sliced sweetbreads sauté, boiled rooster combs, sliced green olives, sliced truffles, and French mushrooms cut in two. Stir into hot Madeira sauce, season well, and fill the croustades.

MARCH 11

BREAKFAST
- Fresh strawberries with cream
- Scrambled eggs with truffles
- Crescents
- Coffee

LUNCHEON
- Hors d'oeuvres variés
- Potato omelet
- Roquefort cheese and crackers
- Hungarian beef goulash
- Coffee

DINNER
- Consommé Du Barry
- Queen olives
- Fillet of sole, Turbigo
- Veal kidney roast
- Carrots in butter
- Mashed potatoes
- Chicory salad
- Fried cream
- Coffee

Scrambled eggs with truffles. Cut a truffle in small dices and put in sauce pan, on the range, with one ounce of butter. When hot add six beaten eggs, a little salt and pepper, one spoonful of cream, and then scramble in the usual manner. Dish up and lay six slices of heated truffles on top.

Potato omelet. Cut a boiled potato in small dices. Put one ounce of butter in a frying pan with the potato, and fry until brown, then add six beaten eggs, season with salt and pepper, and cook into an omelet in the usual manner.

Consommé Du Barry. Boil a cauliflower in salt water. When done cut the tips of the flowers from the stems and add to boiling consommé.

Fillet of sole, Turbigo. Cut the fillets from a sole, and remove the skin. Spread with fish force meat, (see [fish dumplings](#)), fold in half, place in buttered sauté pan, season with salt and pepper, add one-half glass of white wine, and boil. When done remove the fish to a platter; add to the gravy in the pan one cup of white wine sauce, boil for ten minutes, and strain. Cut the tail of a lobster in slices, heat them and lay on top of fillets and cover with the sauce.

Carrots in butter. Wash and peel three dozen small French carrots, and boil in two quarts of salted water. When done drain off the water, add two ounces of sweet butter, and simmer for two minutes. Sprinkle with a little chopped parsley.

Fried cream. One quart of milk, one-half pound of sugar, the yolks of eight eggs, four ounces of flour, and one-half of a vanilla bean. Boil the milk with the vanilla bean. Mix the sugar, flour and the yolks of the eggs, and then pour into the boiling milk. Continue cooking, stirring all the time until stiff. Then pour into a flat pan in a layer about three-quarters of an inch thick, allow to become cold, and then cut into two inch squares. Roll in flour, then in beaten egg, and finally in cake, macaroon, or bread crumbs, and fry in swimming lard until brown. Serve dusted with powdered sugar, or with a lump of sugar covered with brandy, and burning.

Beef tongue, Parisian style. Wash a fresh beef tongue, put in a pot, cover with hot water, add a cup of white wine vinegar, two carrots, two onions, a bay leaf, a few cloves, a crushed garlic clove, some thyme, the green tops of a bunch of celery, and some salt. Simmer slowly for three hours, or until when pricked with a fork it has the consistency of jelly. Then peel and trim. Reduce the broth, and make a brown gravy, adding a glass of Madeira wine. In another pan boil a dozen or so small onions. Glacé and simmer them in plenty of butter, but do not brown, add a can of mushroom heads and quarter of a pound of salt pork that has been boiled and diced, and simmer again. Add two tablespoonfuls of minced parsley and a wine glass of sherry, then mix with the brown Madeira sauce. Put the whole tongue on a platter, and pour the sauce over it.

MARCH 12

BREAKFAST
- Stewed rhubarb
- Boiled eggs
- Rolls
- Coffee

LUNCHEON
- Grapefruit with maraschino
- Fried tomcods, Tartar
- Broiled honeycomb tripe
- Celery root, field and beet salad
- Lyonnaise potatoes
- Cherry tart   Coffee

DINNER
- Potage Lamballe   Radishes
- Bass, Dijonaise
- Roast chicken
- Fonds d'artichauts, Feypell
- Julienne potatoes
- Sliced tomatoes, French dressing
- Vanilla ice cream
- Cakes   Coffee

Bass, Dijonaise. Put four fillets of bass in a buttered pan, season with salt and pepper, sprinkle with two finely-chopped shallots, add one-half cup of water, cover, and put in hot oven for fifteen minutes. Then place the fillets on a platter, and reduce the broth until nearly dry, add one spoonful of French mustard and two cups of cream sauce, and boil for two minutes. Add some chopped chives, and pour over the fish.

Fonds d'artichauts, Feypell. (Artichoke bottoms, Feypell). Remove the leaves, and trim the bottoms of twelve boiled artichokes. Cut six of them into one-half inch squares. Prepare one cup of purée of fresh mushrooms and one-half cup of grated cheese. Put in a sauté pan one ounce of fresh butter, and when hot add the cut-up artichoke bottoms, and season with salt and pepper. Fry until of a light golden yellow color, then add the grated cheese, mix well, add the mushrooms purée, and boil for a minute or two. Finally stir in the yolk of an egg, mixing quickly, and a little chopped parsley. Cover thickly the six whole artichoke bottoms with this filling, place on a buttered dish or pan, lay a thin slice of raw bacon about an inch and a half long on top of each, and put in the oven and bake. Serve as a vegetable course with Madeira or tomato sauce, or as a garnish, plain.

Canapé St. Francis. Trim small pieces of toast, and cut in fancy shapes, or circular. Spread with caviar. Place a slice of tomato on top and over this strips of caviar. Place on lettuce leaves that have been dressed with French dressing mixed with finely-chopped herbs.

Potatoes Ritz. Allow one large potato for each individual. Peel, and cut into half-inch dices. Boil in salt water for ten minutes, drain, and brown with butter. When done the potatoes should be in small free pieces, and browned on all sides.

MARCH 13

BREAKFAST　　　　　　　　　　　LUNCHEON

Grapefruit marmalade
Buckwheat cakes
Breakfast sausages
Maple syrup
Rolls   Coffee

Eggs gastronome
Calf's brains au beurre noir
Persillade potatoes
Hearts of lettuce, French dressing
French pastry   Coffee

DINNER

Toke Point Oysters, mignonette
Potage Mongol
Ripe California olives
Fillet of sole, Villeroi
Roast loin of lamb, mint sauce
Asparagus Polonaise   Potato salad
Savarin aux fruits   Coffee

SUPPER

Yorkshire buck

Coffee

Eggs gastronome. Boil six eggs until hard, remove the shells, and cut in two lengthwise. Chop up the yolks and put in a bowl. Chop very fine one can of French mushrooms, and add to the yolks, season with salt and pepper, add the raw yolk of one egg, one-half cup of fresh bread crumbs and a little chopped parsley, and mix well. Fill the hard-boiled whites with this filling, put on a platter, cover with brown gravy and bake in oven.

Calf's brains au beurre noir. Put two calf's brains in cold water and leave for one hour; then remove the reddish-black outside skin with the fingers, and put again in fresh cold water so the blood will run out, and the brains remain white after being cooked. Now put in a casserole two quarts of water, a heaping spoonful of salt, one-half glass of vinegar, two onions, one-half of a carrot, and a bouquet garni. Boil for five minutes, and then add the brains and boil for two minutes, then let it stand in the hot broth for about one-half hour. Then remove the brains, cut in two lengthwise and lay on a platter, sprinkle with salt and fresh-ground black pepper, one spoonful of French capers, and a little chopped parsley, chives and chervil. Put in a frying pan three ounces of sweet butter and cook until very dark brown, nearly black; and pour over the brains. Then put in the same pan one-third of a cup of vinegar, let it become hot, and pour over the brains also.

Potatoes persillade. Cut two dozen potatoes to the shape of a small egg. Put in a pot, cover with cold water, add a spoonful of salt, and boil slowly so they will not break. When they are nearly soft drain off the water, add one ounce of butter, cover, and simmer until the butter is melted. Then sprinkle with chopped parsley.

Fillet of sole, Villeroi. Put the fillets of a large sole in a buttered pan, add some salt and a glass of milk, bring to a boil, and then set on the side of the stove for ten minutes; then remove the fish to a platter. Mix in a cup one spoonful of flour and one spoonful of butter; add this to the broth in the pan from which the fish has been removed, and boil for five minutes; then add one cup of cream, and two ounces of sweet butter and whip well until melted, season with salt and pepper, and strain over the fish.

Asparagus Polonaise. Put four pounds of boiled fresh asparagus, (for four persons), on a platter. In a frying pan put three ounces of fresh butter, and one-half cup of fresh bread crumbs, and fry until the crumbs are golden yellow. Then pour over the tips of the asparagus, sprinkle with a little pepper and chopped parsley. A hard-boiled egg chopped fine, may be added if desired.

Boiled fresh asparagus. Fresh asparagus should be peeled very thin with a sharp knife, and well washed. If to be served hot, put in boiling salt water over a hot fire about twenty minutes before serving. They should not be cooked in advance. If to be served cold, as soon as the asparagus is done pour a glass of cold water over them so they will not continue cooking and become too soft. Allow to cool in the broth, and before serving lay on a towel or napkin to allow the water to drip off.

MARCH 14

BREAKFAST
Baked beans, Boston style
Brown bread
Buttermilk
Coffee

LUNCHEON
Omelet with oysters
Veal chops, sauté in butter
Purée of salad
Camembert cheese, crackers   Coffee

DINNER
Little Neck clams
Chicken okra soup
Salted almonds
Aiguillettes of bass, Massena
Vol au vent Toulouse
Roast capon, giblet sauce
Stewed asparagus   Château potatoes
Endives salad
Parfait Napolitain
Assorted cakes   Coffee

Purée of salad. (Vegetable). Boil in salted water, lettuce or any other kind of green salad. When done drain off the water and press through a fine colander. Add butter and a little cream.

Aiguillettes of bass, Massena. Put four fillets of bass in a buttered pan, season with salt and pepper; add one-half glass of white wine and one-half glass of stock, bouillon, fish broth or water, cover with buttered paper, and put in oven to bake. When done place the aiguillettes on a platter and cover with the following sauce: Heat one and one-half ounces of butter in a sauce pan, add one spoonful of flour and allow to become brown, add the fish broth left from cooking the bass, one spoonful of meat extract, and one-half spoonful of Worcestershire sauce. Boil for ten minutes, then add one-half teaspoonful of essence of anchovies, and strain through cheese cloth. Boil one dozen clams and cut in two; cut half of the tail of a lobster in small squares, and six heads of mushrooms cut in two. Put all of this in the strained sauce, and season well.

Giblet sauce. Clean the giblets of chickens, turkeys, or other fowl, boil in salt water, and chop. Put in casserole two chopped onions, and two ounces of butter, and simmer for ten minutes, or until soft and yellow. Then add one tablespoonful of flour, and simmer again until brown. Add the gravy from a roast, the chopped giblets and a little of the water the giblets were boiled in. Cook for half an hour, season with salt and pepper and chopped parsley. A little sherry wine may be added before serving, if desired.

Stewed asparagus. Cut up some asparagus tips and cook in a casserole in salt water until soft. Mix a spoonful of flour and one ounce of butter and add to the asparagus, with some of the water used for boiling. Use only enough water to cover the asparagus. Sprinkle with chopped parsley and pepper, and serve in a deep dish.

White bean soup. Soak a quart of beans over night. Put in a vessel with four quarts of water, or a mild soup stock. Add a half pound of lean bacon, and a shinbone, if desired. Start to boil rapidly, then remove to back of stove and cook for several hours until the beans drop to pieces. Skim from time to time. Meanwhile chop very fine an onion, a carrot and a stalk of celery, and simmer in butter until they take on a slightly brown color. Add a spoonful of flour, a potato cut in small dices, and the water from the beans. Strain the beans, and to the purée add the cooked vegetables; cut the bacon in small pieces, and cook all together for twenty minutes. Season with salt, pepper and chopped parsley.

MARCH 15

BREAKFAST
  Bananas with cream

  Scrambled eggs with asparagus tips

  Toast
  Coffee

LUNCHEON
  Crab salad

  Consommé in cups   Cheese straws

  Fried whitebait, rémoulade

  Lamb chops   Sauté potatoes

  Escarole and chicory salad

  Roquefort cheese, crackers   Coffee

DINNER
  Pot au feu
  Loin of pork, baker's oven style
  Mashed turnips
  Celery root and field salad
  Fancy ice cream
  Assorted cakes   Coffee

Fried whitebait. Wash the whitebait well and dry on a towel or napkin. Roll in milk, then in flour, and fry in very hot swimming lard, just enough to make them crisp. Lay them on a napkin, sprinkle with salt, and garnish with fried parsley and quartered lemons. Serve brown bread and butter sandwiches and sauce Tartar or rémoulade.

Pot au feu. Put in a pot one brisket of beef; or five pounds of short ribs of beef; two gallons of cold water, and a handful of salt. Bring slowly to a boil and skim well, so the broth will remain clear. When the boiling point is reached add two whole carrots, two turnips, three stalks of leeks, one stalk of celery, a bouquet garni, one small head of Savoy cabbage, and two large onions, all well washed. Bring to the boiling point again, cover, and put on the side of the stove where it will simmer slowly. The vegetables will be done before the meat, so when they are cooked remove them and throw out the bouquet garni. Let the beef cook until very soft. Cut the vegetables, with the exception of the onions, in thin slices; and when the beef is done strain the broth over the vegetables. Give it another boil, season well, add some chopped chervil, and serve with toasted bread crusts, separate.

The boiled beef may be served as an extra course, usually after the soup, if no fish is served.

Loin of pork, baker's oven style. For a large family, take eight pounds of pork ribs, season with salt and pepper, rub with a piece of garlic thoroughly, and put into a stoneware pot. Cut six large potatoes in strips lengthwise and one inch square, slice three onions and add, with three pints of water, a bay leaf and two cloves, to the meat. Your baker will bake it for you in a brick oven, and it will be a dish quite different from the usual roasted pork. If necessary, put it in your own oven, baking for not less than four hours with a slow, even fire. However, it is preferable to have it baked in a brick oven.

Fried chicken, Vienna style. Cut a chicken in six pieces; two legs, two wings, and two pieces of breast. Season with salt and pepper, roll in flour, then in beaten eggs, and finally in fresh bread crumbs. Put in a sauté pan in two spoonfuls of hot butter, and fry. When done dish up on a platter, garnish with corn fritters, and serve sauce suprême separate.

Peas, farmer style. Shell enough peas to make two cupsful. Take twelve firm large asparagus tips, an onion, a firm head of lettuce cut fine, six small French carrots cut in two, three ounces of butter, a pinch of salt and one of sugar. Add enough water to cover, and simmer slowly until all the vegetables are thoroughly done.

MARCH 16

BREAKFAST
 Grapefruit
 Fried eggs
 Dry toast

LUNCHEON
 Sardines, vinaigrette
 Paprika schnitzel with spätzel
 German apple cake

English breakfast tea   Coffee

DINNER

Blue Point oysters on half shell
Purée paysanne
Pompano sauté, meunière
Tame duckling, apple sauce
Young beets in butter
Sweet potatoes sauté
Waldorf salad
Lemon pie
Coffee

Sardines, vinaigrette. Remove the skins from a can of sardines, and arrange on a platter, on a lettuce leaf. Sprinkle with salt and fresh-ground black pepper, pour a spoonful of vinaigre and one of olive oil over them, and sprinkle with chopped parsley. Garnish with a lemon cut in half, two hard-boiled eggs cut in two, some chopped onion on a small leaf of lettuce, and another small leaf filled with small French capers.

Purée paysanne. (Soup). Slice a carrot, an onion, a turnip, one-half of a stalk of celery, two stalks of leeks, three leaves of cabbage, one-half pound of squash or other fresh vegetable such as asparagus or tomatoes. Put them in a vessel with one-half pound of fresh peas, and one-quarter pound of fresh Lima beans. Cover with two quarts of bouillon and cook until soft. Strain through a fine colander, put back in the vessel, bring to a boil, season with salt and pepper, add two ounces of butter and mix well.

Young beets in butter. Cut some young boiled beets in thin slices, put in sauté pan with butter, season with salt and pepper, and simmer for a few minutes.

Fillet of sole, Villeroi. Put the fillets of a large sole in a buttered pan, add some salt and a glass of milk, and bring to a boil, then set on side of stove for ten minutes. Then remove the fillets to a platter. Mix in a cup one spoonful of flour and one spoonful of butter, and add this to the milk broth in the pan, which has been kept boiling, and cook for five minutes. Then add one cup of cream and two ounces of sweet butter, whip well until melted, season with salt and pepper, and strain over the fish.

Sponge cake. One-half pound of sugar, six yolks of egg and six whole eggs, one-half pound of flour, and flavoring. Beat the eggs and yolks and sugar over a slow fire until blood warm. Then remove and continue beating until cold and very light and spongy. Then add the flour and vanilla, or other flavoring, and mix lightly. Put into paper-lined moulds or pan, and bake in medium hot oven. Serve with powdered sugar dusted on top, or frosted.

Caroline cake. (Chocolate or coffee). Make a dough as for cream puffs, and dress on a pan in drops about quarter the size as for regular cream puffs. Bake in a moderate oven; when done make a hole in the bottom of each with a pointed stick, and fill with pastry cream, or sweetened whipped cream. Place on a wire grill about one-quarter inch apart, and glacé with chocolate or coffee icing. Let the icing dry, and serve in paper cases.

MARCH 17

BREAKFAST
- Fresh strawberries with cream
- Boiled eggs
- Dry toast
- Chocolate with whipped cream

LUNCHEON
- Eggs Princesse
- Chicken sauté, Hongroise
- Mashed potatoes
- Lettuce salad
- Brie cheese and crackers
- Coffee

DINNER
- Little Neck clams

Consommé Camino
Fillet of bass, Menton
Roast leg of lamb
String beans
Château potatoes
Chiffonnade salad
Fancy ice cream
Assorted cakes
Coffee

Eggs Princesse. Put some purée of fresh mushrooms in the bottom of small croustades, lay a poached egg on top, and cover with sauce Périgueux.

Chicken sauté, Hongroise. Joint a chicken and put in a sauté pan with two ounces of butter, season with salt and a little paprika, simmer for five minutes; then add a sliced onion and simmer slowly for ten minutes with the cover over the pan. Then add a cup of cream and cook for four minutes, and add one-half cup of cream sauce. Remove the chicken to a platter, pour the sauce over it, and garnish both ends of the platter with macédoine of vegetables.

Macédoine of vegetables. Macédoine is a mixture of vegetables, and may be obtained in cans, but is easily made at home. If the canned sort is used drain off the juice, put in casserole in cold water, bring to a boil, and then drain off the water, season with salt and pepper, and simmer for a minute or so. To make macédoine, use equal parts of carrots, turnips, string beans, cut in squares about one-quarter inch in diameter, and peas and flageolet beans. Boil each separately in salt water, and mix afterwards, season with salt and pepper and one ounce of butter, and simmer as above. Flageolet beans come in cans, or dry like dry peas. They may be omitted if desired.

Consommé Camino. Boil one-quarter of a pound of macaroni in salt water; when soft, drain, and cool in cold water. Then cut in small pieces about one-half inch in length, and serve in a quart of consommé. Serve grated cheese separate.

Fillet of bass, Menton. Cut four fillets of bass; and prepare some fish dumpling mixture. Spread some of the mixture over the fillets, and fold in half, place in buttered sauté pan, add a little salt and one-half glass of white wine, cover with buttered paper, and place in oven for fifteen minutes. Dish up on a platter and cover with white wine sauce.

Beans, Normandy. Soak two pounds beans over night, then put to boil with three pints of water, sliced carrot, a yellow turnip, an onion, and a bouquet garni, season with salt, and cook for an hour. Put two big spoonfuls of butter and a spoonful of flour in a pan, and make a creamy sauce by adding the water from the beans. Now fill a baking dish; first a layer of sliced potatoes mixed with minced onions, then the semi-cooked beans, then potatoes, and so on until filled. Then add half a glass of white vinegar and bake until the potatoes are done, by which time the beans will be done also.

MARCH 18

BREAKFAST
  Baked apple with cream
  Fried hominy
  Bar le Duc jelly
  Rolls
  Coffee

LUNCHEON
  Oranges en suprême
  Clam broth in cup
  Fillet of sole, Orly
  Tripe and oysters in cream
  Baked potatoes
  Diplomate pudding
  Coffee

DINNER
  Cream of celery
  Pompano, Café Anglaise
  Chicken sauté, Portugaise
  Fresh asparagus, Hollandaise

Julienne potatoes
Romaine salad
Sponge cake
Compote of mixed fruits
Coffee

Orange en suprême. Slice six oranges, put in bowl with three spoonfuls of powdered sugar and two ponys of Curaçao, let stand for thirty minutes, and serve in suprême glasses.

Fillet of sole, Orly. Roll four fillets of sole in the form of cigars, put in flour, then in beaten eggs, and finally in bread crumbs, and fry in hot swimming lard. When done lay on napkin, garnish with quartered lemon and fried parsley, and serve tomato sauce separate.

Diplomate pudding. Take sponge, or any kind of left over cake and cut in small pieces, using enough to fill a pudding mould. Add about a teaspoonful of chopped candied fruit to each person. Make a custard with one quart of milk, six eggs and a half pound of sugar; pour over the cake in the mould, and bake. Serve with brandy sauce with some chopped candied fruit in it.

Pompano, Café Anglaise. Put four small whole pompano and four fillets of pompano in a buttered sauté pan, and season with salt and pepper. Put in another vessel one dozen clams and one dozen oysters, with their own juice, and bring to a boil. Then strain the broth over the pompano and boil until done. Remove the fish to platter, reduce the broth, then add one cup of cream sauce and one cup of white wine sauce, and strain. Put the oysters and clams and one dozen écrevisse tails in the sauce and pour over the fish. The sauce should be well seasoned. Garnish with small fried fillets of sole.

Small fried fillets of sole. Cut fillets of sole into small strips about one-quarter inch thick and two inches long, roll in milk and then in flour, and fry in hot swimming lard. When crisp take out of the fat and sprinkle with salt. Serve with Tartar sauce as fried fillet of sole, or use as a garnish for fish.

Chicken sauté, Portugaise. Joint a chicken and season with salt and pepper. Put in sauté pan one spoonful of olive oil and one of butter, heat, add the chicken, and sauté until golden yellow; then add three finely chopped shallots and simmer for a minute; add one can of French, or one-half pound of fresh mushrooms sauté in butter; two peeled and quartered tomatoes, or the same amount of canned ones, using the pulp only, and simmer for five minutes. Add one cup of tomato sauce, and simmer again for five minutes. Put the chicken on a platter, pour the sauce with its garnishing on top, and sprinkle with chopped parsley. A little chopped garlic may be added at the same time as the chopped shallots, if desired.

MARCH 19

BREAKFAST
Preserved figs with cream
Scrambled eggs with parsley
Puff paste crescents
Oolong tea

LUNCHEON
Eggs Du Barry
Boiled ham, Leonard
Stewed tomatoes, Brazilian
Mashed potatoes
Roquefort cheese, crackers   Coffee

DINNER
Velvet soup
Ripe California olives
Skatefish au beurre noir
Baked chicken with rice
Chiffonnade salad
Bavarois à la vanille
Assorted cakes   Coffee

Baked chicken with rice. Put in a saucepan a fat hen with all of its fat, cover with hot water, season with salt, and when it comes to a boil, skim off the foam but leave the fat. Add a soup bouquet with the addition of some spices and a bay leaf. When the hen is half done, which will be in about an hour, remove the bouquet, and add a cup of washed rice. Boil until the rice is nearly done, by which time it has absorbed most of the broth; then put into a porcelain baking dish and bake until brown.

Eggs Du Barry. Line an egg cocotte with a forcemeat made of truffles and beef tongue, drop an egg into this, set the dish in hot water and cook in the oven for from five to ten minutes. When done cover with hot purée of cauliflower.

Purée of cauliflower. Boil a head of cauliflower in salted water. When soft drain off the water and press the cauliflower through a fine colander. Season with salt and pepper, and add a spoonful of cream sauce.

Forcemeat of truffles and tongue. Put through a fine sieve two slices of beef tongue, then add a truffle chopped fine, the yolk of one egg, and a little pepper.

Boiled ham, à la Leonard. Soak a smoked ham in cold water for twelve hours, after having cut off the handle bone and shortening the hip bone. Set on the fire and bring to the boiling point very gradually, then drain off the water, and replace with water of tepid warmth. Add four or five carrots, two bay leaves, a small bunch of thyme, sage and basil and a bunch of celery tops, all tied in a bunch. Season with mace, cloves and pepper berries, let it come to bubbling heat, and then set on back of stove, where it may simmer at an even temperature. When done; allowing about a quarter of an hour for each pound of meat; peel, and serve with a sauce made of some clear soup stock, Madeira sauce, three spoonfuls of molasses and a spoonful of French mustard. The ham should be basted frequently while cooking.

Velvet soup. Mince fine the red part of a few carrots, stew them with butter, salt, sugar and a little broth. When done strain through a sieve. Put a quart of clear broth on to boil, mix in four tablespoonfuls of tapioca, let it stand for twenty-five minutes on the side of the fire, skimming well. At the last minute before serving add the carrot purée, season, boil up once or twice more, and serve in a tureen.

Tomato stew, Brazilian. Dice a piece of white bread and simmer with two ounces of butter, slightly browning it. Add four peeled tomatoes and a can of Lima beans with the water drained off, and season. Then add a half cup of chicken broth or well-flavored stock, and simmer for twenty minutes.

MARCH 20

BREAKFAST
  Strawberries with cream
  Boiled eggs
  Dry toast
  Coffee

LUNCHEON
  Raisin cocktail
  Consommé in cups
  Broiled shad roe with bacon
  Cold roast beef
  Cole slaw
  French pastry
  Coffee

DINNER
  Purée Céléstine
  Radishes
  Paupiettes of bass
  Mutton chops, Milanaise
  Peas, farmer style
  Homemade apple pudding
  Coffee

Broiled shad roe with bacon. Season four shad roes with salt and pepper, lay in oil, and broil. When done place on platter and cover with maître d'hôtel sauce. Lay eight crisp-broiled slices of bacon on top of the roe, and garnish with quartered lemon and parsley.

Purée Céléstine. Same as purée of potatoes.

Purée of potatoes. Peel four well-washed white potatoes, and cut in pieces. Put in a vessel with one quart of stock and two cut-up stalks of leeks, and boil until done. Then strain through a fine sieve, put back in vessel, season with salt and pepper, add two ounces of butter, and stir well until the butter is melted.

Paupiettes of bass. Cut four fillets of bass about one-quarter of an inch thick, two inches wide and six inches long. Lay them flat on the table and spread with a thin layer of fish dumpling preparation. Roll them up and place standing in a buttered sauté pan, season with salt and white pepper, add one-half glass of white wine and one-half cup of stock or hot water, cover with buttered paper, and put in oven for fifteen minutes. Then remove the fish to a platter, reduce the broth until nearly dry, add one pint of white wine sauce, strain, and pour over the fish. Decorate the tops with chopped hard-boiled eggs, chopped parsley, and lobster corals chopped very fine.

Lobster corals. In lobsters may be found a solid red substance which is known as lobster corals. Remove the corals from a boiled lobster, put on a covered plate and dry on the stove until very hard. Chop fine, and use for decorating fish, salads, etc. It will keep a long time in a dry place.

Raisin cocktail. Soak seedless raisins in sherry wine for fifteen minutes, then put a heaping spoonful in each cocktail glass. Make a sauce of tomato ketchup, tobasco sauce, celery seed, and the juice of two lemons; allowing the latter to a half pint of ketchup. Add a few chopped almonds, fill the glasses and chill, or serve with ice around the glasses.

Homemade apple pudding. Fry four sliced apples in a little butter and a pinch of powdered cinnamon. Cut half of a five cent loaf of milk bread into small squares, mix with the apple and put in a pudding mould. Mix half a pound of sugar with four eggs and one quart of milk, strain, and pour into the mould. Allow to soak for a half hour, and bake in a moderate oven.

Maraschino sauce for iced pudding. One-half pint of cream, one pony of maraschino, one-quarter of a pound of sugar. Beat all together until a little thick, and serve very cold.

MARCH 21

BREAKFAST
　Oatmeal and cream
　Broiled kippered herring
　Baked potatoes
　Rolls
　Coffee

LUNCHEON
　Canapé St. Francis
　Eggs, Carême
　Hot buckwurst with potato salad
　Limburger cheese and crackers
　Coffee

DINNER
　Potage Eliza
　Terrapin, Maryland
　Beef tongue, Parisian style
　Potatoes Ritz
　Beans, Normandy
　Hearts of lettuce
　Savarin au kirsch
　Coffee

Broiled kippered herring. Kippered herring may be obtained in cans. Dip in oil and broil very lightly, cover with maître d'hôtel sauce, and garnish with lemon and parsley.

Eggs, Carême. Butter a shirred egg dish, crack two eggs into it, and season with salt and pepper. Slice a truffle and a few canned mushrooms, mix with a little cream sauce, and pour over the eggs. Bake in oven.

Hot buckwurst. Secure the buckwurst from your butcher, lay them in boiling water for ten minutes, but do not let the water boil after they have been put in it.

Potage Eliza. Same as potage santé.

How to boil terrapin. Put two live terrapin into boiling water and leave for two minutes. Then remove the outer skin from the feet, neck and head, with a towel. Put the terrapin in a kettle with two quarts of cold water, an onion, a carrot, a bay leaf, and one clove, and boil until the feet are soft. The time required depends upon the age of the terrapin, some being cooked in fifteen minutes, and others requiring two or three hours. When done open the shell, take out all the meat, and the liver, removing the gall from the latter with scissors. Remove the tail and claws and head. Cut up the legs in inch-long pieces, or at the joints, as preferred. Reduce the broth by boiling down to about a cupful, and put in a jar with the meat, and add a whiskey glass of sherry wine. The terrapin is then ready to prepare in any style desired.

Terrapin, Maryland. Put one cup of terrapin, prepared as above, in a flat pan, add a little grated nutmeg, salt and pepper, and half a glass of dry sherry. Boil until half reduced, then add a cup of thick cream, boil, and thicken with the yolks of two eggs, a quarter of a cup of thick cream and an ounce of butter beaten together. Heat, but do not boil. Serve in chafing dish, with dry sherry, and toast on the side.

Terrapin, Jockey club. Same as Terrapin, Maryland. Before serving add two ponies of Cognac and six slices of truffles.

Terrapin, Baltimore. One cup of the prepared terrapin without the liver. Put in saucepan with salt, pepper, nutmeg, celery salt, and a glass of dry sherry. Boil for five minutes. Mash the liver in a salad bowl, add the yolks of two raw eggs, one ounce of sweet butter, and strain through a fine sieve. Add a cup of brown sauce to the simmering terrapin, then add the liver prepared as above, pouring in gradually. Heat barely enough to thicken. Before serving add half a glass of dry sherry.

MARCH 22

BREAKFAST	LUNCHEON
Fresh raspberries with cream	Grapefruit en suprême
Scrambled eggs with smoked beef	Crab meat, Monza

    Rolls   Loin of pork, baker's oven style
    Coffee   Field salad
                                                 Prune soufflé   Coffee

DINNER

    Little Neck clams
    White bean soup
    Salt codfish, Nova Scotia
    Fried chicken, Vienna style
    Corn fritters   Mashed potatoes
    Romaine salad
    Diplomate pudding, glacé   Coffee

Crab in chafing dish. Mince a shallot onion and brown slightly with two spoonfuls of butter. Add a spoonful of flour, mixing well, then add a half pint of sweet milk, and stir to a smooth cream. Add the meat of a California crab (or six eastern crabs) and a tablespoonful of sherry. Place toast, cut in fancy shapes, on a deep platter, and cover with the crab. This is a favorite way of preparing crab.

Crab meat au gratin. Shred the meat of one crab, mix with a cup of cream sauce and a little paprika, or Cayenne; or if this is too strong use white pepper. Fill individual baking dishes, and sprinkle the top liberally with grated Parmesan cheese. Bake in an oven until the top is an even brown.

Crab meat, Gourmet. Put a quarter of a pound of picked shrimps in a saucepan, add one ounce of butter and one-half whiskey-glassful of dry sherry wine. Simmer for five minutes, then add the meat of one crab, prepared Monza.

Crab meat, Suzette. Bake four good-sized potatoes, and cut off one side like the cover of a box. Scoop the insides out with a spoon, and fill with the meat of one crab prepared in cream. Sprinkle some grated Parmesan or Swiss cheese on top, and bake in oven until nice and brown. Serve on napkins, garnished with parsley in branches and quartered lemons.

Oysters or crab, à la Poulette. If for oysters, boil them in their own liquid for about five minutes. If the small California oysters are used boil for half that time. Into this liquid of, say, a pint of oysters, stir a heaping teaspoonful of corn starch mixed with a half pint of white wine. Then beat the yolks of two eggs with half a cup of cream, and stir slowly into the above, add two large spoonfuls of butter, and keep on the stove but do not let it boil. Finally squeeze in the juice of half a small lemon. If crab is used, cut the meat in small pieces, and make the sauce in the same manner, but instead of beginning with the juice of oysters for the foundation of the sauce, begin with a cup and a half of cream and water in equal proportions, thicken with corn starch, then add the yolks of eggs, etc., as above. The oysters or the crab meat should be added last.

Crab meat, à la Louise. Have the crab meat thoroughly chilled, and allow one crab to three or four people, according to the size of the fish. Use small fancy fish plates, or salad plates. Lay on each plate some slices of the white hearts of firm heads of lettuce. Lay on top some canned Spanish pimentos, using the brilliant red variety, which is sweet. On top of this place the crab meat, taking care not to break it too small. Over all pour French dressing made with tarragon vinegar, well-seasoned with freshly-ground black pepper.

MARCH 23

BREAKFAST
- Hominy and cream
- Ham and eggs
- Rolls
- Coffee

LUNCHEON
- Sardines with lemon
- Clam broth in cups
- Sand dabs, meunière
- Plain boiled potatoes
- Asparagus, vinaigrette
- Edam cheese and crackers
- Coffee

DINNER
  Potage Coquelin
  Radishes and olives
  Broiled pompano, Havanaise
  Leg of mutton, Clamart
  Rissolées potatoes
  Lettuce and tomato salad
  Fancy ice cream
  Assorted cakes
  Coffee

SUPPER
  Eggs Pocahontas

Eggs Pocahontas. Fry six strips of bacon, and two dozen California, or one dozen Blue Point, oysters. Scramble ten eggs and mix with the above. Season well.

Potage Coquelin. Garnish purée of pea soup with chicken and leeks cut Julienne style, and boiled in broth.

Broiled pompano, Havanaise. Serve broiled pompano with a Colbert sauce, to which has been added two red peppers (pimentos), cut Julienne style. Pour the sauce over the fish, or serve separate, as desired.

Leg of mutton, Clamart. Roast leg of mutton garnished with purée of peas. Serve brown gravy.

Lettuce and tomato salad. Put the leaves of a head of lettuce in a salad bowl. In the center place four peeled and sliced, or quartered, tomatoes. Pour one-half cup of French dressing or mayonnaise over the tomatoes.

Crab meat, Belle Helene. Put six whole tomatoes in hot water for fifteen seconds, then cool immediately, and remove the skins. Cut a hole in the tops the size of a quarter of a dollar, scoop out the insides, season the inside of the shells with salt and pepper, fill with crab meat Monza, and bake in oven for ten minutes. Serve on platters, garnished with parsley and quartered lemons.

Prune soufflé. Wash a cupful of prunes thoroughly, and soak them over night. Boil them in the water in which they were soaked, flavoring with half of a vanilla bean, and sweetened with a cupful of sugar. When done pour off and save the juice. Strain the pulp through a colander or wire sieve, making a good firm purée, and about a cupful in quantity. Whip the whites of six eggs until dry, then whip in the prune pulp, and bake in the same manner as an omelette soufflé. Bake on a platter, formed into a symmetrical mound; or in a buttered pudding mould. Serve hot or cold, with a sauce made of the flavored juice in which the prunes were cooked, or it may be served with whipped cream. Other fruit may be prepared in the same manner, if desired.

Salt codfish, Nova Scotia. Soak two pounds of salt codfish in cold water for six hours. Then put in casserole in one pint of water, boil for ten minutes, drain, add one pint of Créole sauce, boil slowly for five minutes, and serve hot with fresh-boiled rice.

MARCH 24

BREAKFAST
  Stewed prunes
  Boiled eggs
  Buttered toast
  English breakfast tea

LUNCHEON
  Crab cocktail, Victor
  Broiled shad roe, ravigote
  Tripe sauté, Lyonnaise
  Château potatoes
  Escarole salad
  Caroline cake
  Coffee

DINNER
  Clam chowder, Boston style
  Fillet of sole, under glass
  Roast chicken
  Julienne potatoes
  Asparagus, Hollandaise

Baked Alaska
Coffee

Broiled shad roe, ravigote. Broil the roe, place on a platter, and cover with a sauce made by mixing one-half cup of maître d'hôtel sauce with two chopped vinegar pickles and one teaspoonful of French mustard.

Fillet of sole under glass. Cut the fillets into pieces two inches square. Into a buttered shirred egg dish put a piece of toast; on top of this place the fish, season with salt and pepper, put three fresh mushroom heads on each portion of fish, add a piece of butter about the size of an egg, and over all squeeze the juice of half a lemon, and sprinkle with finely-chopped parsley. Cover with a glass cover, such as used for mushrooms, put in a moderate oven and cook for twenty minutes; being careful that the oven is not hot enough to burn the toast. Then take from the oven, pour velouté sauce and a spoonful of white wine over each portion, and return, to cook for another five minutes. Any other fish may be substituted for sole, if desired.

Clam chowder, Boston style. Put fifty clams, with their liquid, into a saucepan and boil for three minutes. Then set the clams aside, strain the broth and return to the fire. Chop fine, a medium-sized onion, and cut into dice four slices of salt pork. Put a piece of butter into a pan, and fry the pork and onion until light brown in color; stir in two tablespoonfuls of flour and cook thoroughly, add the clam juice, a half pint of rich soup stock, and the same amount of cream, a couple of diced potatoes, and a bit of thyme if the flavor is liked. Cook for about ten minutes. Chop the clams, and add last of all, as they do not require much cooking. Just before serving add a few hard crackers broken into bits.

Crab cocktail, Victor. Place a boiled crab on ice and chill thoroughly, then remove the meat, taking care not to break the pieces more than necessary. Make a sauce with three-quarters of a cup of tomato ketchup, a teaspoonful of Worcestershire sauce, two tablespoonfuls of tarragon vinegar, and a good pinch of freshly-ground pepper. Mix with the crab meat, fill the cocktail glasses, place them in cracked ice, and serve.

Baked Alaska. (Individual). Slice some sponge cake about one-half inch thick, and cut with a round cutter two inches in diameter. Place the discs of cake on a silver platter, put a ball of vanilla cream in the center of each, and cover with meringue paste. Make the meringue with the whites of four eggs, beaten well and mixed with one-half pound of powdered sugar. Use a pastry bag with a fancy tube, and cover carefully; dust with powdered sugar, and bake in a very hot oven for a couple of minutes. Put a French cherry on top of each before serving.

MARCH 25

BREAKFAST
Fresh strawberries with cream
Bacon with eggs
Rolls
Coffee

LUNCHEON
Grapefruit with cherries
Chicken broth with rice
Crab meat, Gourmet
Rolled veal, Huguenin
Onions, Hongroise
Camembert cheese, crackers   Coffee

DINNER
Toke Points on half shell
Potage Esau
Shrimps with mushrooms
Rack of lamb, mint sauce
String beans   Potato croquettes
Chiffonnade salad
Peach Melba
Assorted cakes   Coffee

Rolled veal, Huguenin. Cut four thin slices of veal and flatten out smoothly. Chop fine two young green onions and two slices of bacon; and crush and chop fine, half of a clove of garlic, add a little pepper, and spread over the veal, roll up tight and tie with a string. In a saucepan put a piece of butter the size of an egg, and the veal, and simmer for three-quarters of an hour, basting frequently. Before serving season with salt and sprinkle with parsley.

Shrimps with mushrooms. Fry two cups of shrimps and half a cup of fresh mushrooms in plenty of butter. Season with nutmeg, salt and pepper, and the juice of half a lemon. Add two spoonfuls of tomato sauce, half a cup of stock, and a few bread crumbs. Sprinkle with chopped parsley.

Onions, Hongroise. Chop fine a large Bermuda onion, cover with water, and cook until tender. Drain, add half a pound of fresh cream cheese, a pint of sweet cream, a large can of pimentos, and a teaspoonful of paprika. Serve in a chafing dish. Do not salt.

Peach Melba. Peel some large fresh peaches, and cook them whole in a light syrup; or use whole preserved peaches. From vanilla ice cream, that is frozen very hard, cut some round pieces about three inches in diameter and an inch thick. Place the ice cream on plates, place a peach on the center of each, and pour Melba sauce over them.

Raspberry Melba sauce. Mix well a half pint of strained raspberry pulp, the juice of one lemon, and half a pound of powdered sugar; place in an earthen pot and let it set over night. Then pack in ice, stir well, add a cup of powdered sugar, and stir every half hour until smooth and thick. Keep in ice until used.

Potage Esau. Same as purée of lentils.

Diplomate pudding glacé. Mix in a bowl one pint of preserved fruit; or fresh fruit that has been cooked in syrup; cut in small dices, add a pony of kirsch and one of maraschino, and allow to macerate for one hour. Beat the yolks of four eggs with a quarter of a pound of sugar and half of a split vanilla bean, over the fire, until light and creamy; then remove from the fire and continue beating until cold. Then add one pint of whipped cream and the prepared fruit, and mix well together. Put in a pudding mould, pack in ice and rock salt, and freeze for about two hours. Serve with cold brandy sauce with chopped fruit in it.

MARCH 26

BREAKFAST
Preserved figs
Omelet with tomatoes
Rolls
Coffee

LUNCHEON
Hors d'oeuvres variés
Sand dabs, meunière
Broiled rump steak
French fried potatoes
Smothered onions
Romaine salad
Eclairs   Coffee

DINNER
Viennese bean soup
Crab meat en Bellevue
Chicken, Tyrolienne
Boiled rice
Asparagus, Hollandaise
Strawberry pie   Coffee

Viennese bean soup. Wash a pint of beans, then put them in water and let them soak over night. Then put in a vessel with three quarts of water and a quarter of a pound of lean salt pork, and cook slowly for three hours, by which time the beans should be done. Meanwhile mince an onion, a large carrot, and a stalk of celery; fry them in butter, but do not brown. Add a spoonful of flour and two cups of the beans, making a thick sauce; add this to the beans in the pot, and cook slowly for another hour. Season to taste, and sprinkle with chopped parsley before serving. Cut the pork in very thin slices, and serve one slice to each plate.

Chicken, Tyrolienne. Joint a tender fowl, and dust lightly with flour. Put into a pan with plenty of butter, and simmer slowly for about fifteen minutes, turning frequently so it will become brown on all sides. Then sprinkle liberally with salt and pepper, add a spoonful of sherry and half a cup of brown gravy, a slice of boiled ham diced fine, and one large tomato cut in small pieces. Simmer slowly again for ten minutes. Dish up on a platter, sprinkle with chopped parsley, and garnish with apples fried in butter.

Peach pie. Slice about five peaches for each pie, add sugar and cinnamon to taste, cover, and finish in the same manner as apple pie. For preserved peaches very little sugar is required.

Apricot, pear and pineapple pies. Make in the same manner as peach pie.

Strawberry pie. Clean and wash the berries, and add three ounces of sugar for each pie. Line the pie plate with dough, and put a handful of biscuit crumbs on the bottom, before putting in the berries. The crumbs will prevent the juice from running.

Raspberry, blackberry, huckleberry, gooseberry, currant, grape and cherry pies, prepare in the same manner as strawberry pie.

English gooseberry pie. Fill a deep china vegetable dish with gooseberries, add one-quarter pound of sugar and two cloves to each individual dish, wet the edges of the dish, cover with pie dough, wash the top with eggs, and bake. When done dust the top with powdered sugar, allow to cool, and serve cream separate.

English huckleberry or currant pie, same as English gooseberry pie.

English rhubarb pie. Remove the outer skin from rhubarb, cut in small pieces, and prepare the same as English gooseberry pie.

English grape pie. Same as gooseberry but use a little less sugar.

MARCH 27

BREAKFAST	LUNCHEON
Sliced oranges	Indian canapé

Omelet with kidneys
Rolls
Coffee

Rack of lamb, jardinière
Lettuce salad
Floating island
Lady fingers   Coffee

DINNER

Cream of chicken, à la Reine   Queen olives
Fillet of rock cod, Nantaise
Sweetbreads braisé, Henri IV
Julienne potatoes
Fresh artichokes, sauce mousseline
Pâté de foie gras   Lettuce salad
Pudding à la Rossini   Coffee

Omelet with kidneys. Make a plain omelet, and before turning over on platter put a small spoonful of kidney stew (see kidney stew), in the center. Put some stewed kidneys at each end of the omelet.

Rack of lamb. Have the butcher cut a rack of lamb consisting of about ten chops. Season with salt and pepper, and put in a small roasting pan with a sliced onion and carrot, and two ounces of butter. Put in a hot oven to roast, basting every few seconds so it will not become dry. If necessary, add a spoonful of water to prevent the vegetables from burning. After twenty minutes remove the lamb to a platter, and add a spoonful of flour to the pan, and simmer for five minutes; then add one cup of stock or hot water, and one spoonful of meat extract. Season, strain, and pour over the rack of lamb. Garnish with fresh watercress.

Rack of lamb, jardinière. Garnish the rack of lamb with a bouquet of peas, and a bouquet of string beans, cauliflower, spring carrots in butter, or any kind of fresh vegetables. Some kind of potatoes, such as Parisian, Julienne, etc., may be added, if desired.

Sweetbreads braisé, Henry IV. Braised sweetbreads with sauce Béarnaise, garnished with Julienne potatoes, and sliced truffles cut in triangles, placed on top of the sweetbreads.

Pudding à la Rossini. Cut six large thin pancakes in strips one inch wide, and line a buttered pudding mould with them, one overlapping the other. Boil a pint of milk, add one-quarter of a pound of flour to it, and stir well to a thick batter; then remove from the fire, whip in one-quarter pound of sugar and two ounces of butter, two ounces of grated cocoanut, the rind of a lemon, and the yolks of six eggs. Beat the whites of six eggs very stiff and add, mixing lightly. Fill the lined pudding mould, and bake in a slow oven for about forty minutes. Serve hot, with orange sauce.

Orange sauce. Boil together one pint of water, one-half pound of sugar, and the grated rind of an orange. While boiling, stir in one teaspoonful of corn starch dissolved in a little cold water, boil for a few minutes, remove from the fire and add the juice of one or two oranges. Strain.

Lemon sauce. Same as orange sauce, using lemons instead of oranges, and in the same proportions.

Fillet of rock cod, Nantaise. Season four fillets of rock cod with salt and pepper, dip in oil and broil. When done place on platter and cover with the following butter: Press six sardines through a fine sieve, mix with two ounces of butter, the juice of two lemons, and some chopped parsley.

MARCH 28

BREAKFAST
  Fresh strawberries with cream
  Boiled eggs
  Dry toast
  Coffee

LUNCHEON
  Matjes herring, potato salad
  Chicken croquettes, cream sauce
  Asparagus tips
  Tapioca pudding
  Coffee

DINNER

        Giblet soup, à l'Anglaise
        Radishes
        Terrapin, Jockey Club
        Baby lamb steak, horticulture
        Escarole salad
        Bavarois noisettes
        Alsatian wafers
        Coffee

Matjes herring. This is an imported salted herring. Lay six herrings in cold water for an hour, and then clean. Put them in a stone pot, add a sliced onion, one-quarter cup of whole black pepper berries, two bay leaves, four cloves, one-half cup of vinegar, two cups of cream, and a little salt if necessary. Allow to stand for a couple of days, and then serve on lettuce leaves, with its own sauce, and with sliced lemon on top.

Baby lamb steak, horticulture. Cut a steak from the leg of a spring lamb, season with salt and pepper, roll in oil, and broil. When done dish up on a platter, cover with Madeira sauce, and garnish with different vegetables, such as peas, carrots, stuffed tomatoes, stuffed peppers, string beans, cauliflower, asparagus tips, artichokes, etc. Arrange the vegetables in bouquets, and use as many kinds as you desire.

Bavarois noisette. The yolks of eight eggs, one quart of milk, one-half of a split vanilla bean, one-half pound of sugar, one-quarter pound of ground hazelnuts, one pint of whipped cream, and five sheets of French gelatine. Boil the milk with the vanilla. Roast the hazelnuts, grind, or chop them very fine, and mix with the yolks of eggs and sugar. Add the boiling milk, and stir over the fire until it thickens, but do not let it boil. Remove from the fire and add the gelatine (which has been washed) in cold water, and stir with a spoon until melted. Allow to become cold, remove the vanilla bean, add the whipped cream, mix well, put in a fancy mould, and set in the ice box for two hours. Serve with whipped cream with chopped hazelnuts in it.

Indian Canapé. Use one hard-boiled egg for each person to be served, and force through a sieve. For six eggs add a quarter of a pound of sweet butter, a half teaspoonful of curry, and beat into a smooth paste. Toward the last add a tablespoonful of cream. Spread over toast, and place a little chopped chutney on top of each.

Pommes d'arbre, 1915 (apple, 1915). Peel and core six apples and cook them in syrup, with the addition of half of a vanilla bean. Drain, and allow to become cold. Make a cream sauce with half a pint of cream, two ounces of sugar, and two sheets of gelatine, and pour over the apples, coating them nice and smooth. Sprinkle the top with nonpareil candies, and place in ice box. Serve in suprême glasses, with vanilla cream in the bottom of the glass.

MARCH 29

BREAKFAST
- Oatmeal and cream
- Broiled kippered herrings
- Lyonnaise potatoes
- Rolls
- English breakfast tea

LUNCHEON
- Omelet with soft clams
- Blood pudding
- Mashed turnips
- Mashed potatoes
- Roquefort cheese and crackers
- Coffee

DINNER
- German lentil soup
- Salted almonds
- Crab meat, au gratin
- Tournedos, Rossini
- Château potatoes
- Chiffonade salad
- Pommes d'arbre, 1915
- Assorted cakes

Coffee

German lentil soup. To a purée of lentils, add before serving, some sliced Frankfurter sausages, and a little bacon cut in small strips and fried.

Quince jelly. To each pound of cut-up quinces add a cup of water, put in a kettle and stew until soft. Then put in a jelly bag to drain, but do not crush. Add a pound of sugar to each pint of liquor, boil gently until the sugar is dissolved, then boil more quickly. Pour into glasses, and when cold cover with paraffine.

Preserved pears. Peel, halve, and remove the cores from Bartlett or Seckle pears. Allow one pound of sugar to each pound of fruit. Put the sugar on to melt, with a few spoonfuls of water. Stick a clove in each piece of fruit, and boil in the sugar until thoroughly done. Put the fruit in glass jars, cover with the syrup, and seal. The rind of one lemon to every five pounds of fruit may be used instead of the cloves, if desired, or both may be used.

Pineapple preserves. Pare and slice the pineapples, then weigh out one pound of cane sugar to each pound of fruit. Put a layer of the slices in a stone jar, sprinkle with the sugar, continue until fruit and sugar are used up, and allow to stand over night. Then remove the pineapple and cook the syrup until it thickens, add the fruit, and boil for fifteen minutes, remove the fruit and let it cool, then put in jars and pour the syrup over it. A very little ginger root boiled in the syrup will improve it.

Citron preserves. Pare some sound fruit, divide into quarters, remove the seeds, and cut in small pieces. To every pound of fruit allow one-half pound of granulated cane sugar. Cook the citron in water until quite clear, then drain through a colander. Melt the sugar with a few spoonfuls of water, and boil until very clear, then put in the drained citron, add two sliced large lemons, a small piece of ginger root, and cook for about fifteen minutes. Fill the jars with the citron, and cover with the syrup.

MARCH 30

BREAKFAST
Honey in comb
Scrambled eggs with chives
Rolls
Coffee

LUNCHEON
Canapé of fresh Astrachan caviar
Saddle of hare, sour cream sauce
Palestine potatoes
Spatzle
Green peas au beurre
French pastry   Coffee

DINNER
Lobster chowder
Ripe California olives
Broiled barracouda
Roast leg of lamb, mint sauce
String beans
Alsatian potatoes
Escarole salad
Biscuit Tortoni
Assorted cakes
Coffee

Scrambled eggs with chives. Make some plain scrambled eggs, and just before serving add some finely-cut chives, mix, and season well.

Sweet potato croquettes. Boil four large potatoes in salt water, when soft, peel, and pass through a sieve. Then put in a casserole, add two ounces of butter, the yolks of three eggs, season with salt and pepper, and mix well. When cold, roll in flour, shape in the form of a large cork, then roll in beaten eggs and bread crumbs, and fry in very hot swimming lard. When nice and brown serve on a napkin.

Palestine potatoes. Sweet potato croquettes formed in the shape of a small pear. When fried, dress on a napkin with the pointed end up, and stick a sprig of parsley in the top.

Alsatian potatoes. Put in a casserole two ounces of butter and one chopped onion, and simmer until golden yellow. Add four potatoes cut in small dices, one bay leaf, one clove, one cup of water, and season with salt and pepper. Cover, and simmer slowly for thirty minutes. Add fresh chopped parsley before serving.

Biscuit Tortoni. Same as biscuit glacé, with the addition of a pony of good maraschino and two ounces of macaroon crumbs. To make the crumbs, crush some dry macaroons and pass through a sieve or colander. Put in round paper cases, filling above the edge, and allow to set in ice box for several hours until frozen. Dip the top of the biscuit in macaroon crumbs before serving.

Saddle of hare, sour cream sauce. Remove the skins from the saddles of two hares, and lard them with thin strips of larding pork. Put them in an agate pan, add a little salt, and one-half cup of whole black peppers wrapped in cheese cloth. Cover with from two to three quarts of sour cream, and stand in a cool place for forty-eight hours. Then put the saddles in a roasting pan with a sliced onion and carrot, and a little butter on top, and roast in a hot oven for about ten minutes, or until brown. Then strain the sour cream, and add little by little to the saddles, while roasting. Baste continually, and after forty minutes you should have a nice brown sauce. Remove the saddles to a platter, reduce the sauce one-half, season with salt if necessary, and a little paprika, strain part over the saddles, and serve the remainder in a bowl.

MARCH 31

BREAKFAST
- Hothouse raspberries with cream
- Browned corned beef hash
- Poached eggs on toast
- Rolls
- Coffee

LUNCHEON
- Grapefruit with cherries
- Frogs' legs, sauté à sec
- Lamb chops
- Watercress salad
- French fried potatoes
- Camembert cheese with crackers
- Coffee

DINNER
- Petite marmite
- Radishes
- Crab à la Louis
- Boiled beef, horseradish sauce
- Boiled potatoes
- Stuffed cabbage
- Hearts of lettuce salad
- Apple water ice
- Cakes
- Coffee

Corned beef hash. Chop an onion very fine and put in a casserole with two ounces of butter. Simmer until the onion is cooked, then add two pounds of boiled corned beef cut in small dices, and one pound of boiled potatoes cut very small, or chopped. Mix well, season with a little pepper, and salt if necessary, add one cup of bouillon, and simmer for ten minutes. Before serving add a little chopped parsley.

Browned corned beef hash. Same as above, but use only one-half cup of bouillon. Before serving put the hash in a frying pan with two ounces of butter, and allow it to brown. Serve in the shape of an omelet.

Corned beef hash au gratin. Make a corned beef hash and put in a buttered, deep, silver vegetable dish, sprinkle with bread crumbs, put a small piece of butter on top, and bake in oven until brown.

Lamb cutlets in papers. Fry the cutlets in a sauté pan, in melted fat pork, turning frequently. Brown only slightly, allowing them to remain rare. Then remove the cutlets, and in the fat simmer some minced onions, mushrooms and parsley for a few minutes. When nearly done add some shredded lean ham. Now prepare some oiled paper, tearing it heart-shaped, lay the cutlet on one half, surrounding it with the minced herbs, with a little on top also; then fold over the paper, creasing the edges together like a hem. Lay on a buttered dish, and set in oven until nicely colored.

Purée of onions (Soubise). Peel and slice one dozen large white onions, put in a casserole with one-quarter pound of butter, cover, and put in oven for about forty-five minutes, or until soft; but do not allow them to become brown. Then drain off the butter and add one pint of thick cream sauce, season well with salt and white pepper, and strain through a fine sieve.